Forests

ISBN 978-1546613657

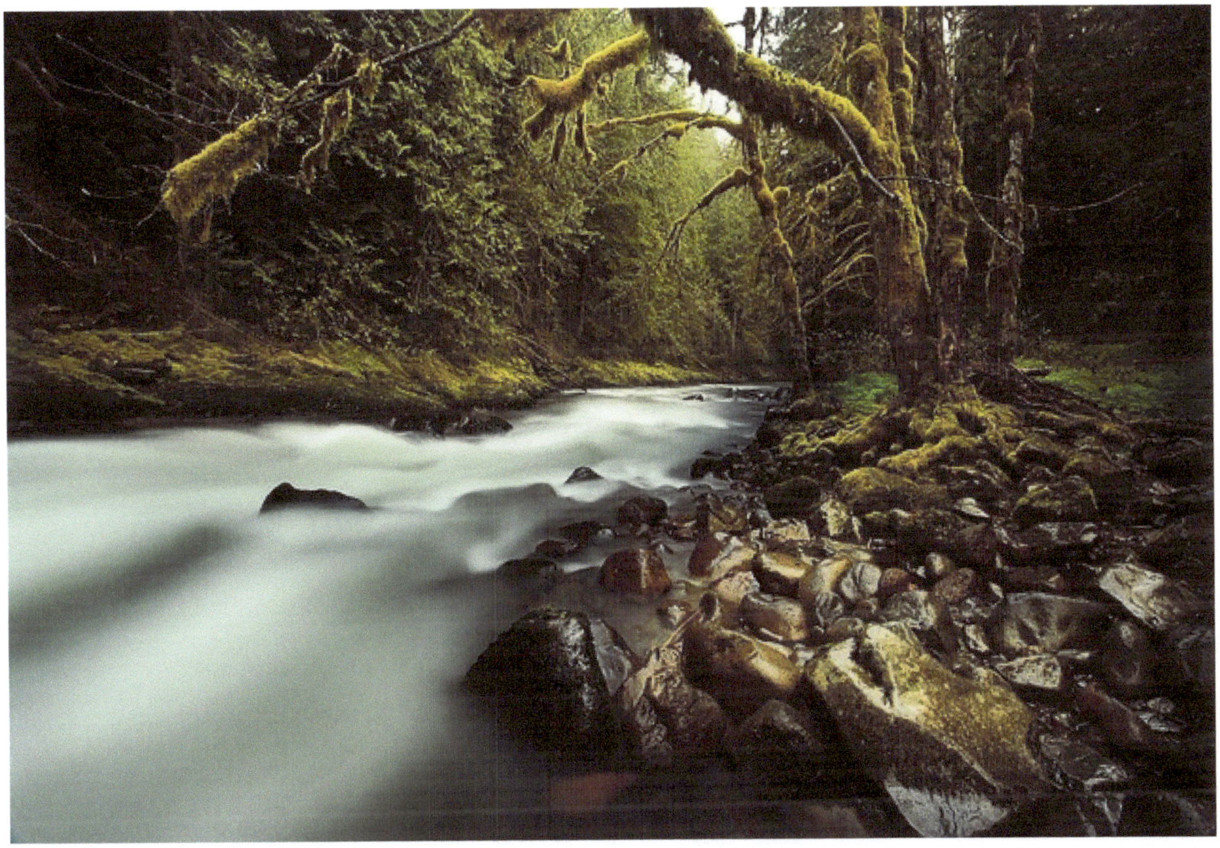

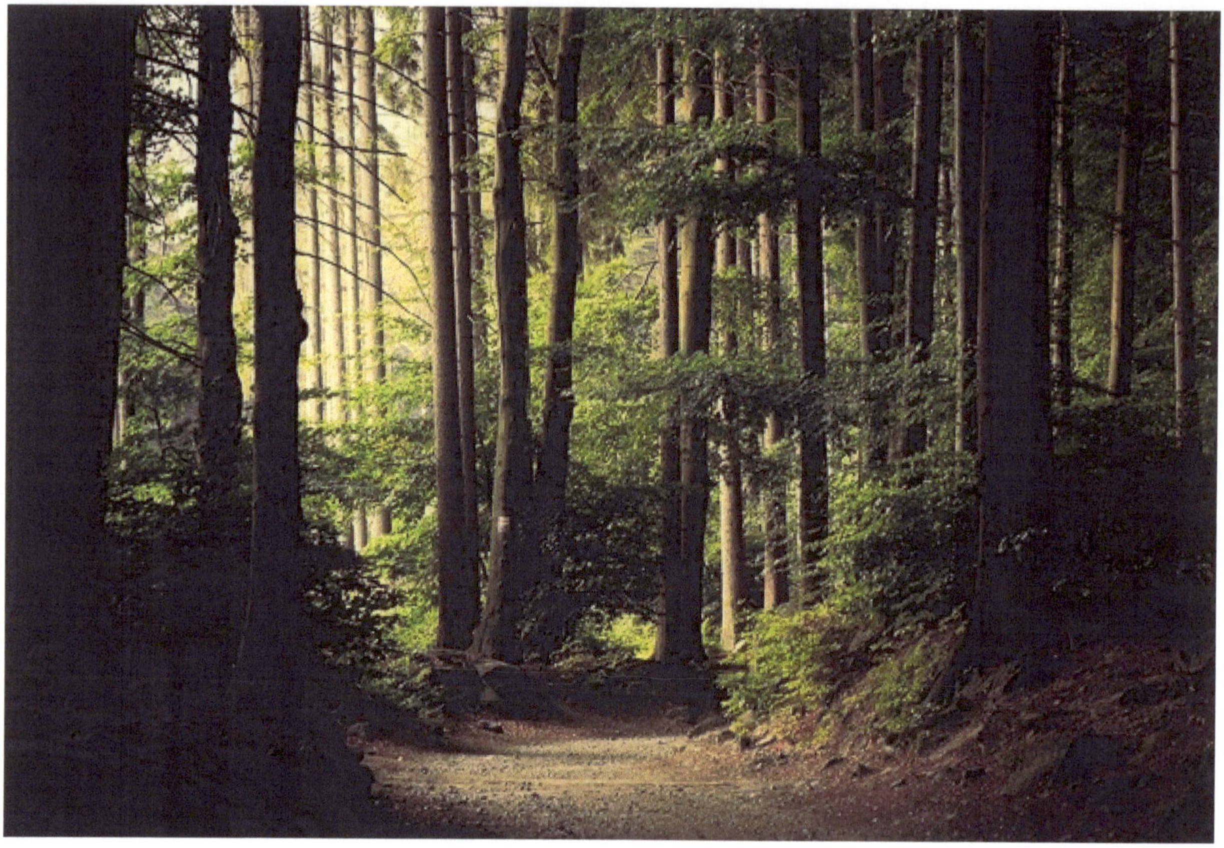

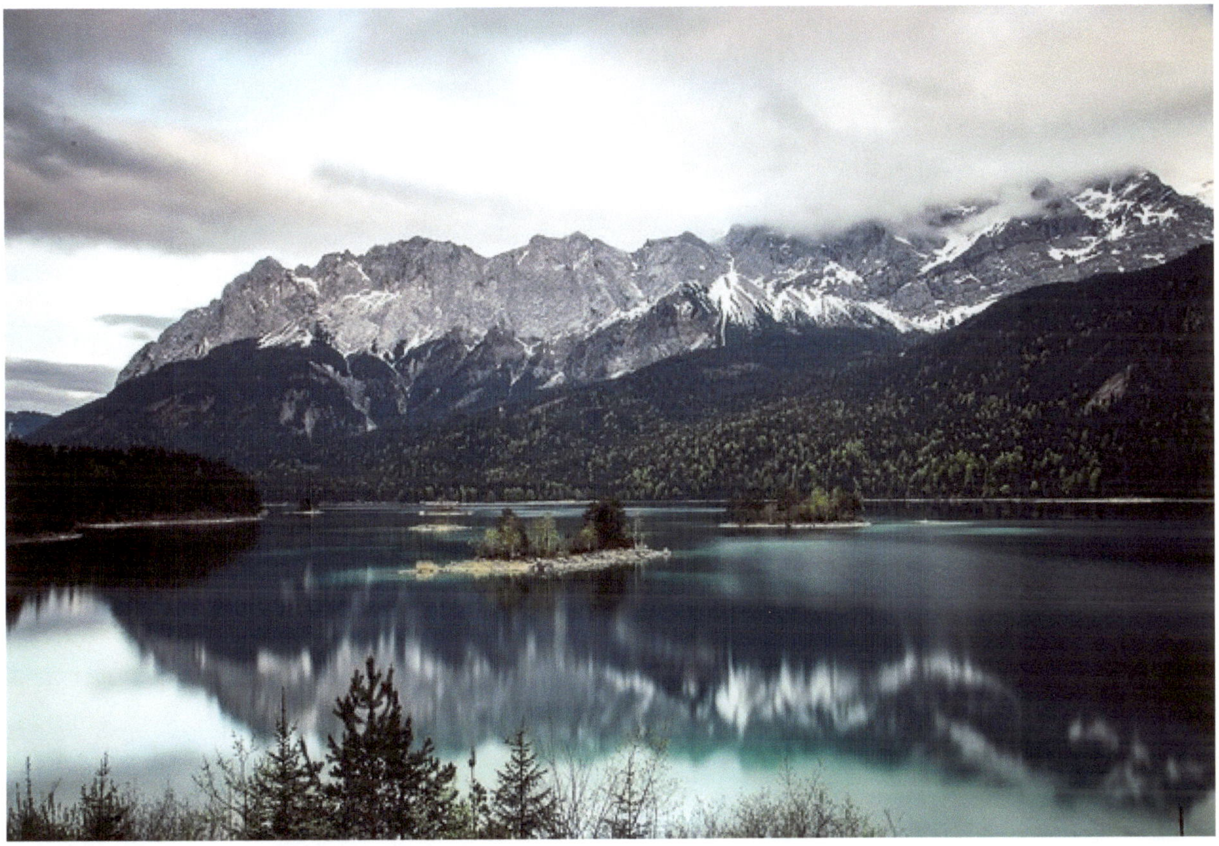

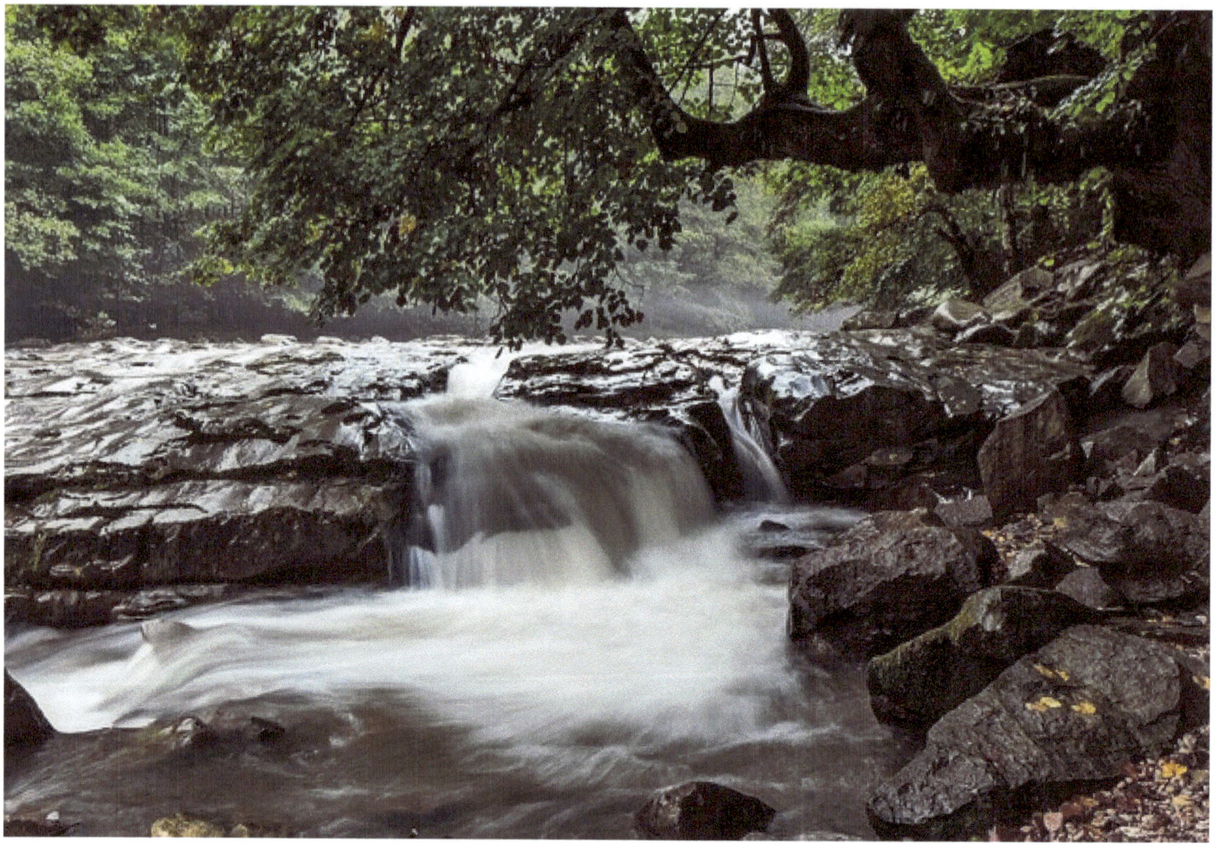

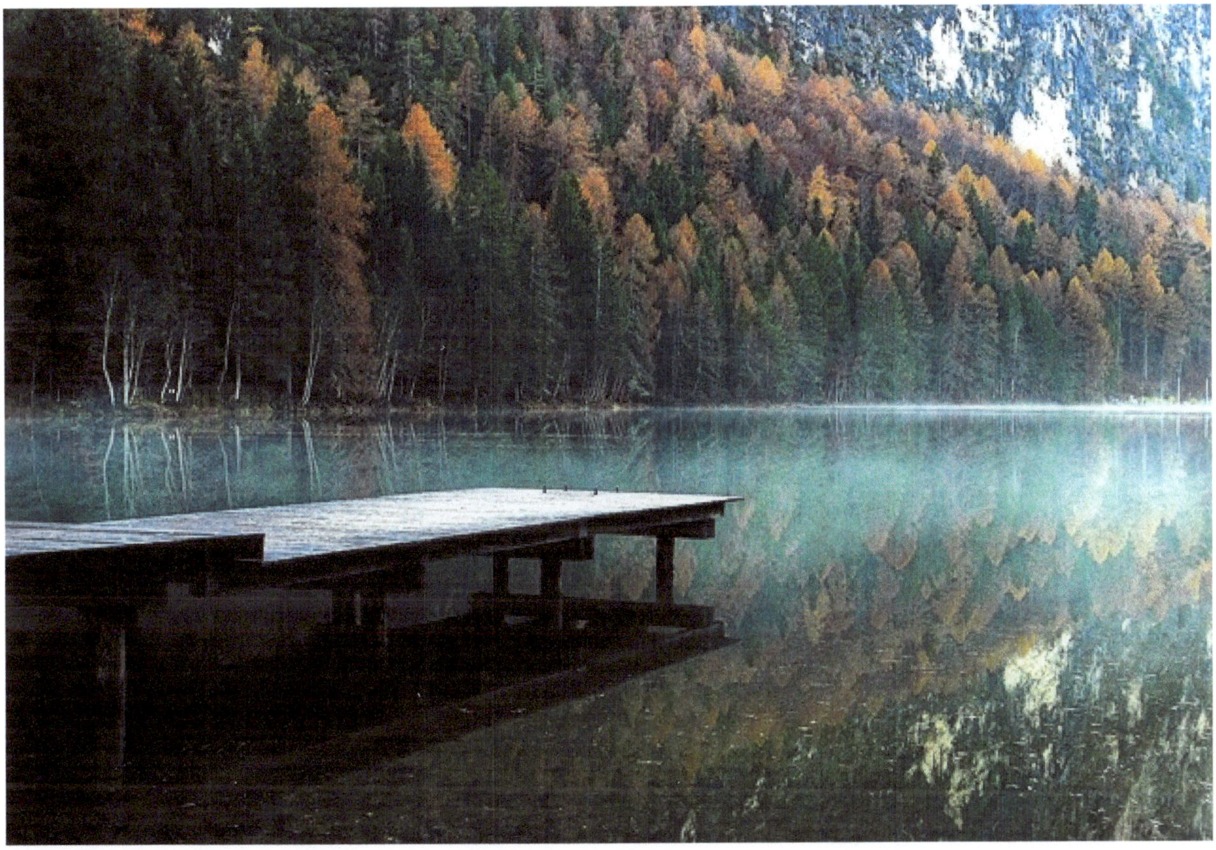

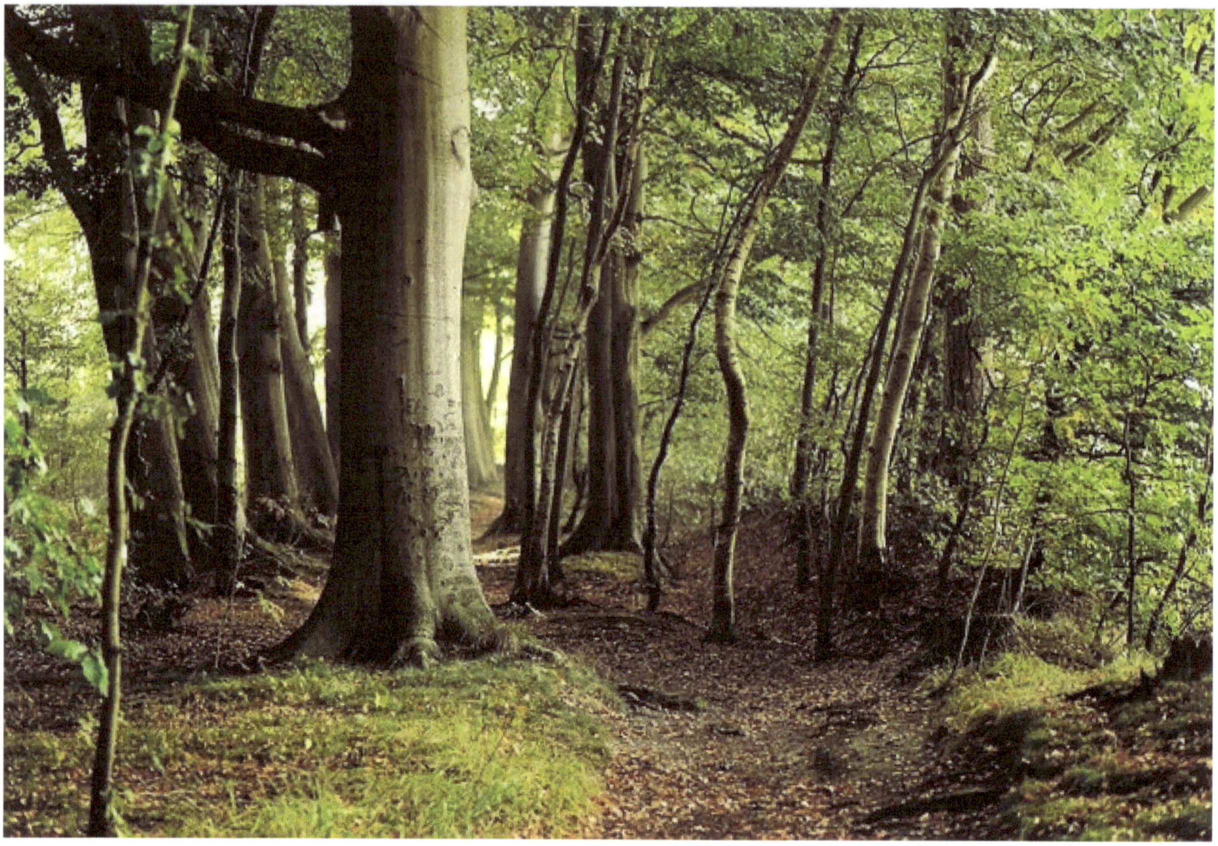

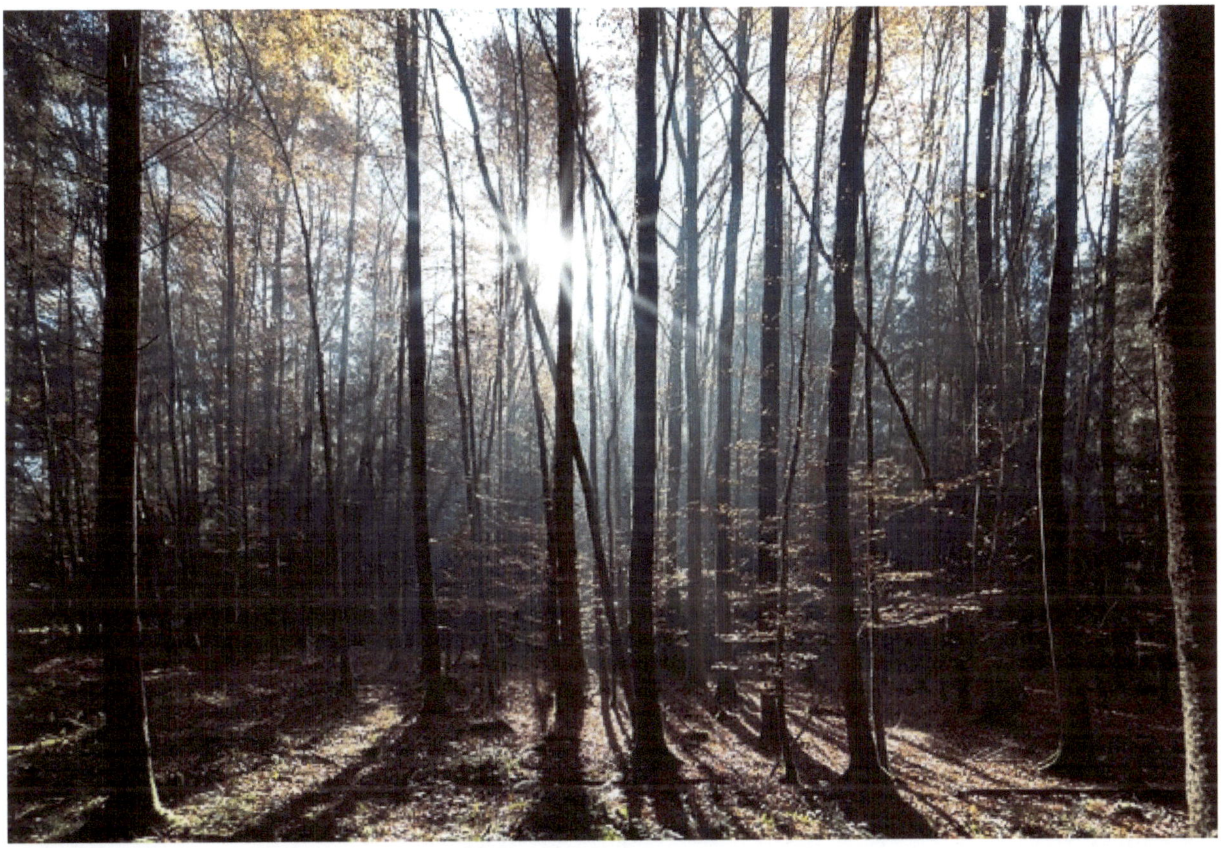

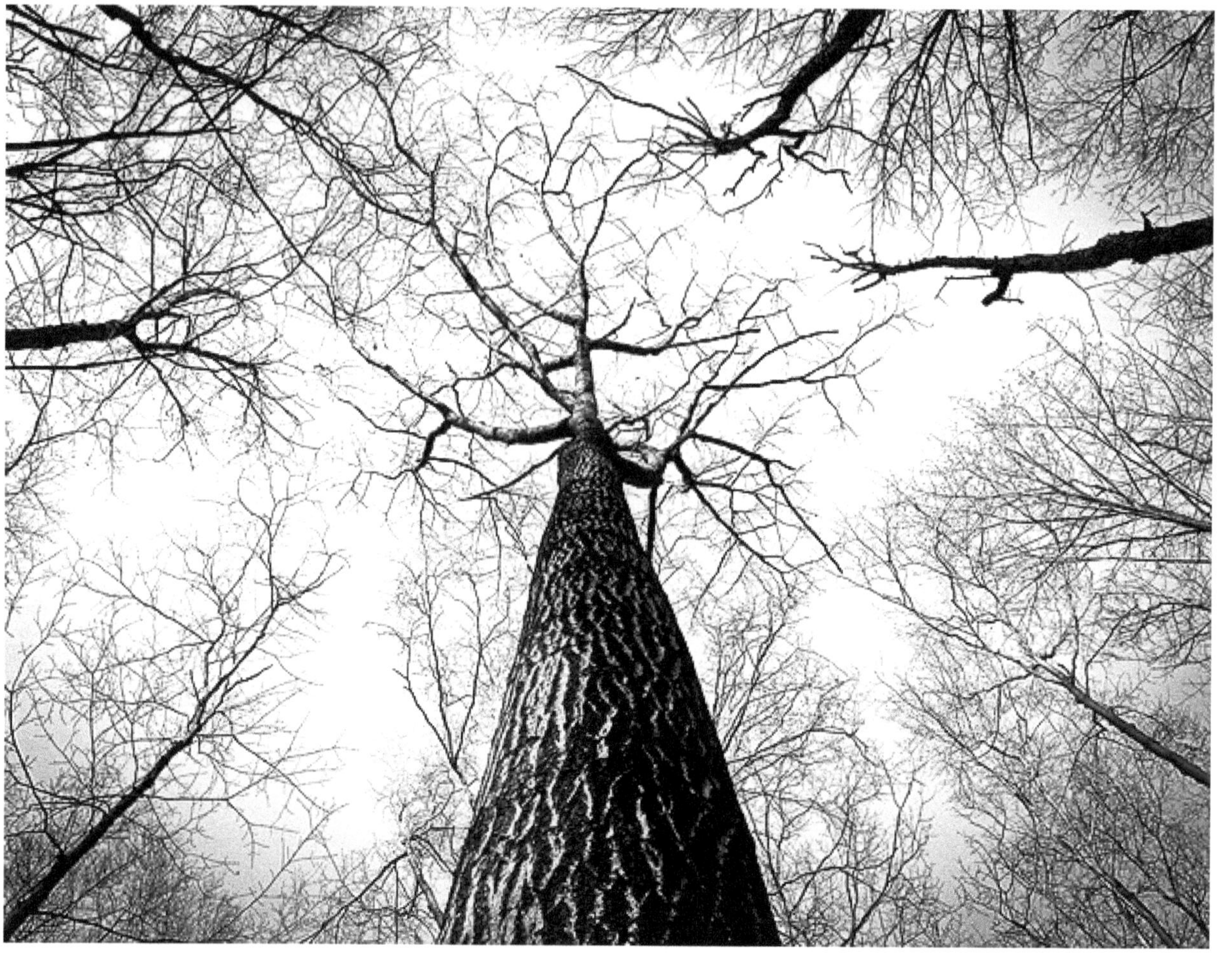

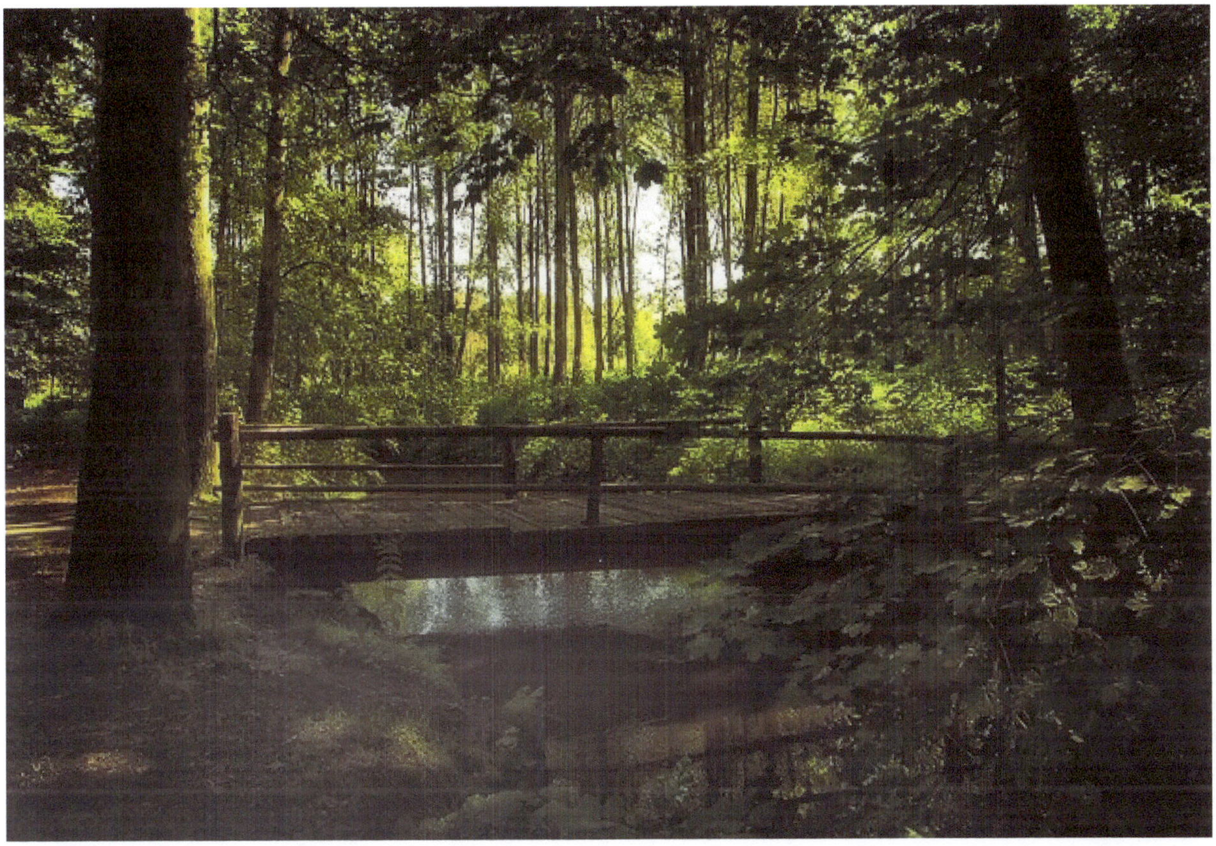

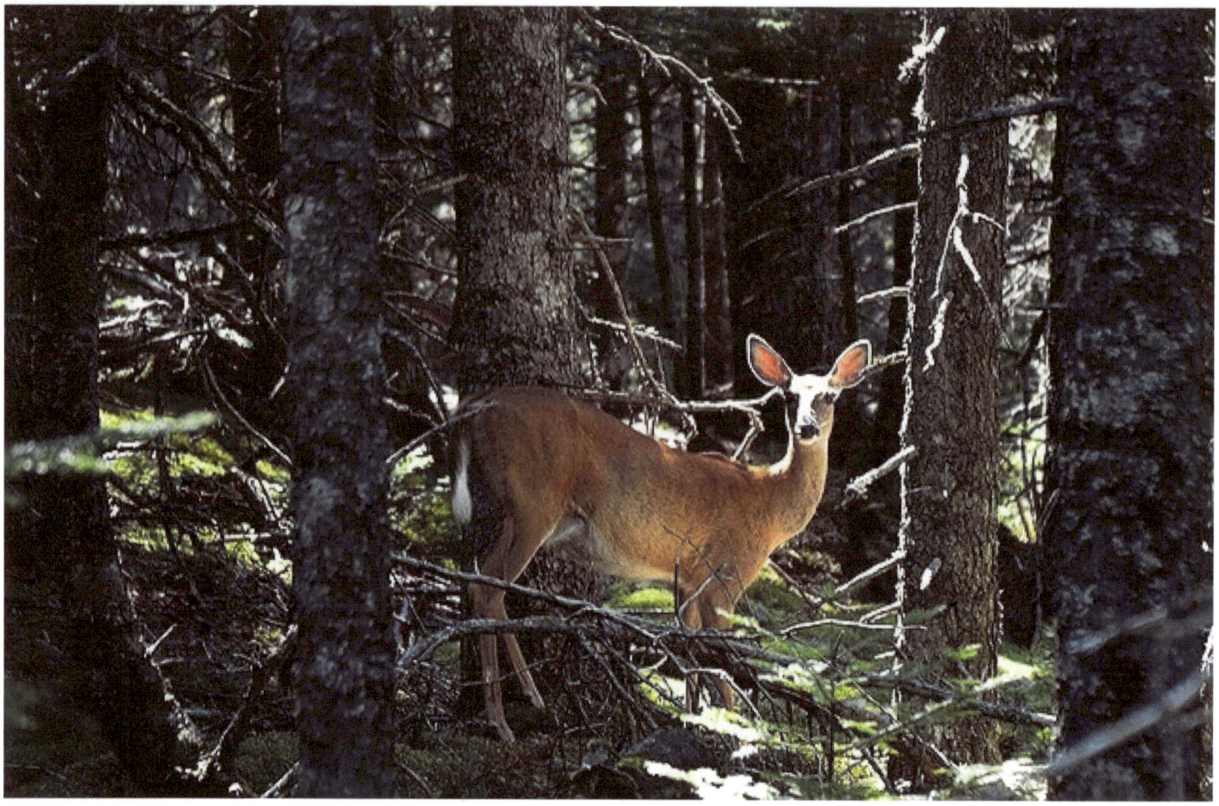

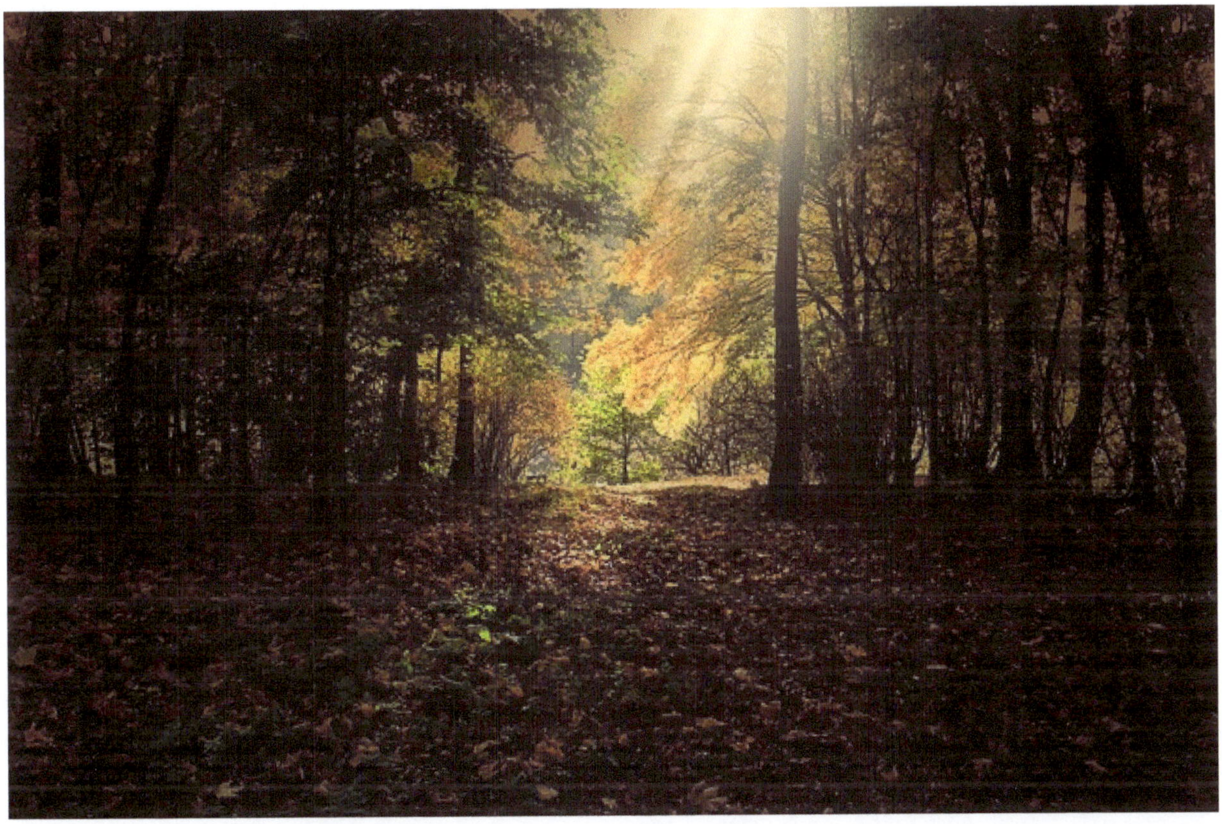

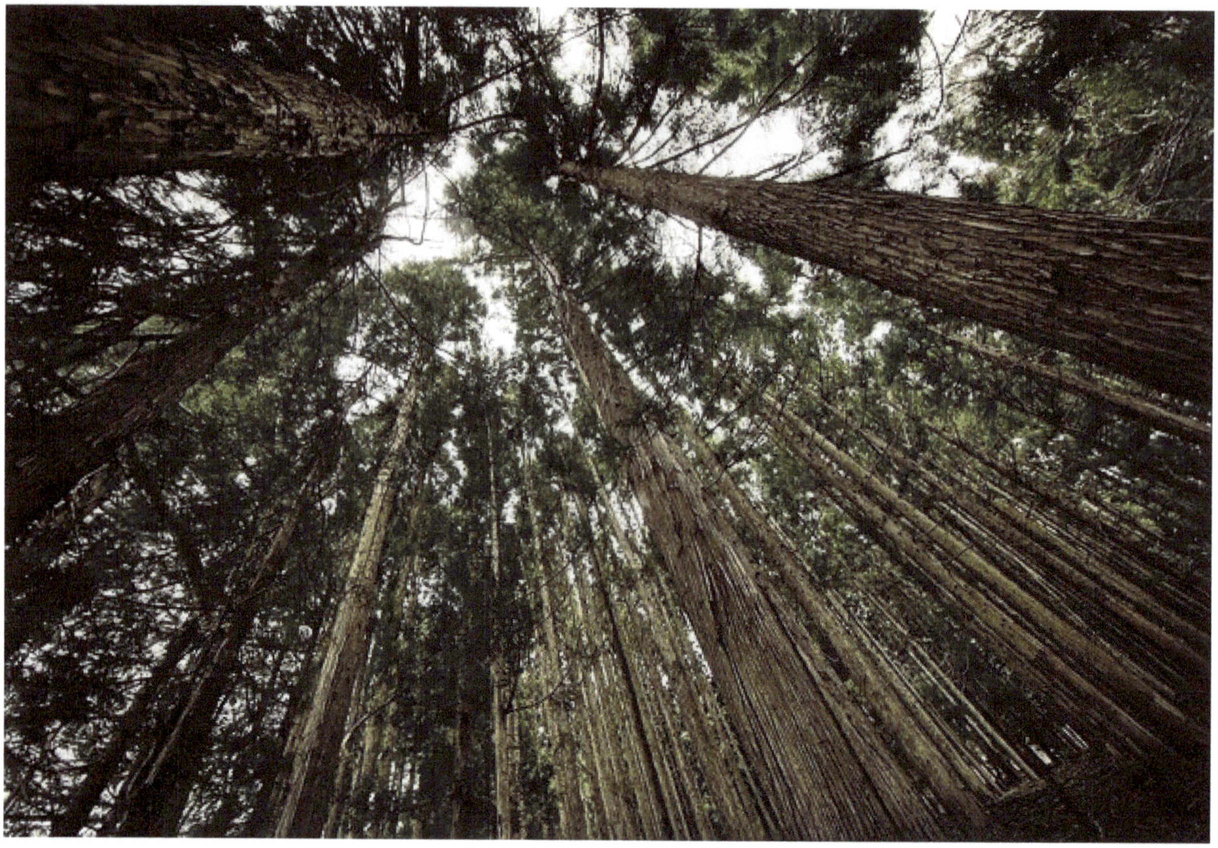

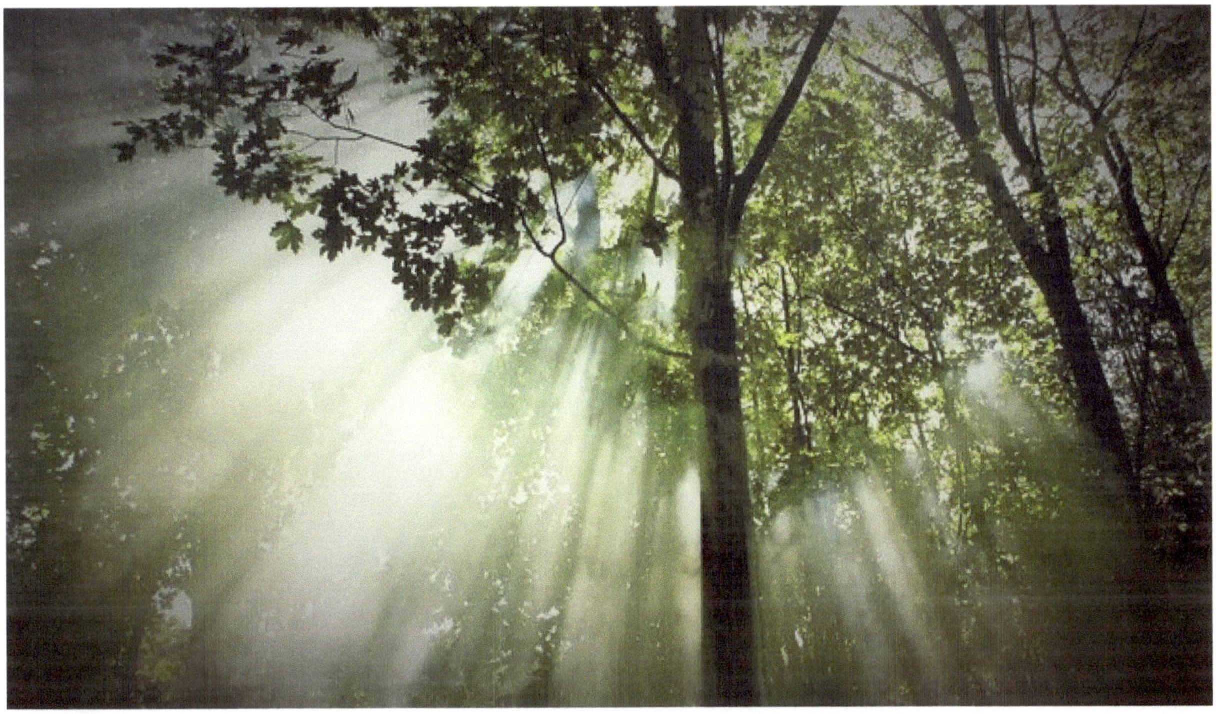

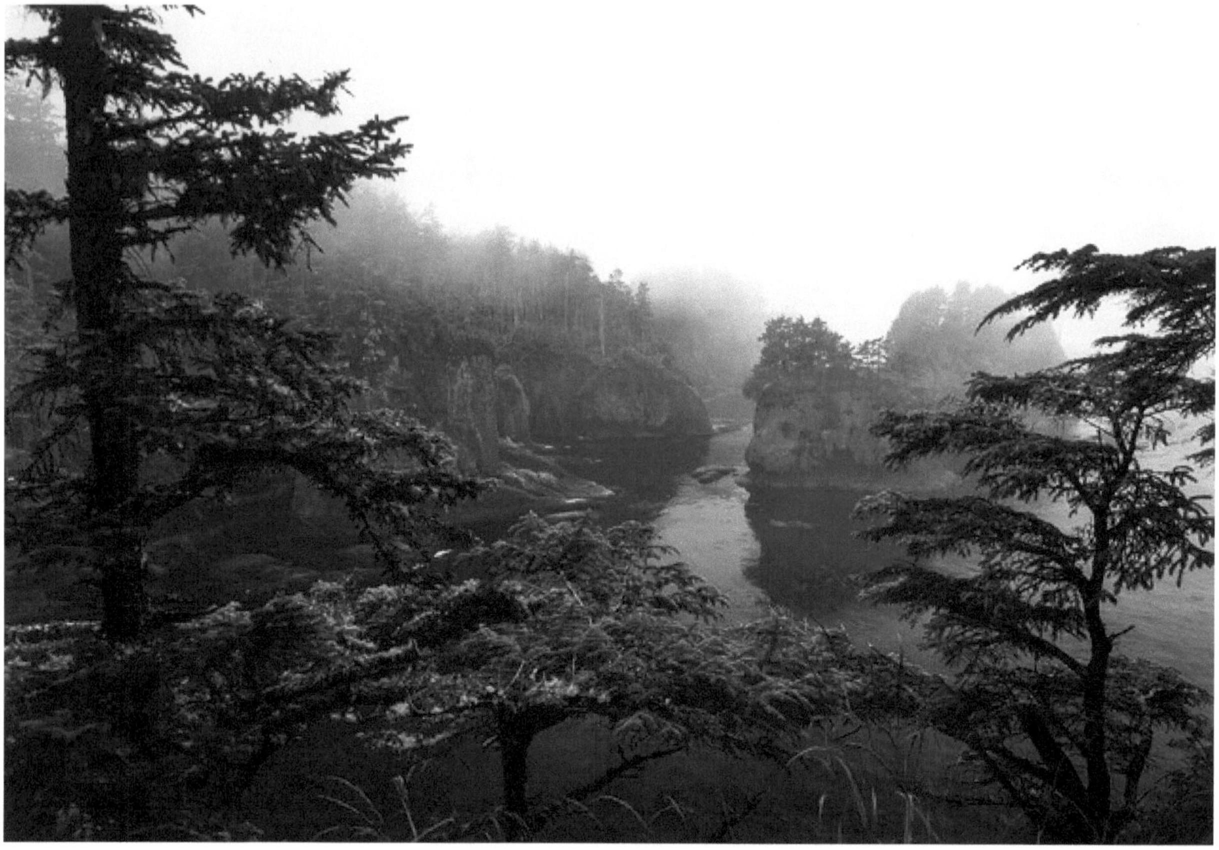

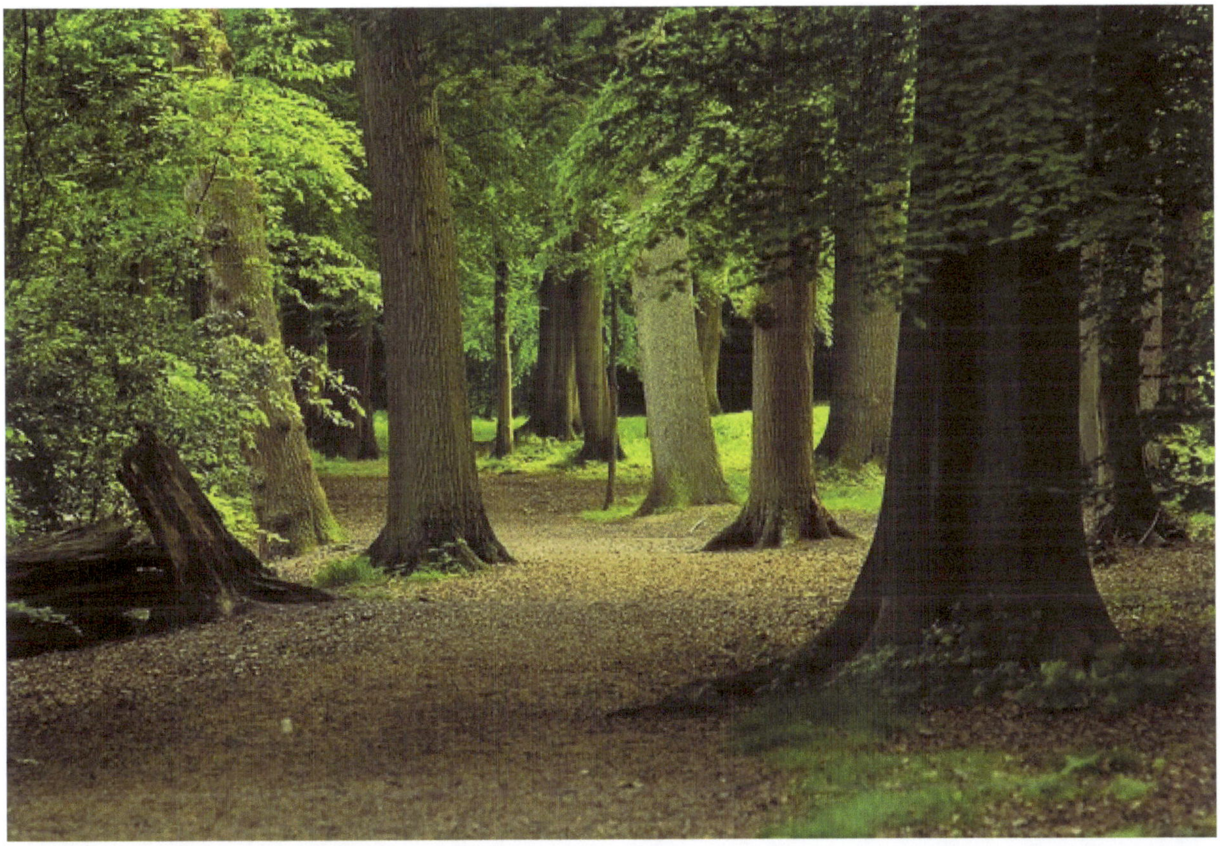

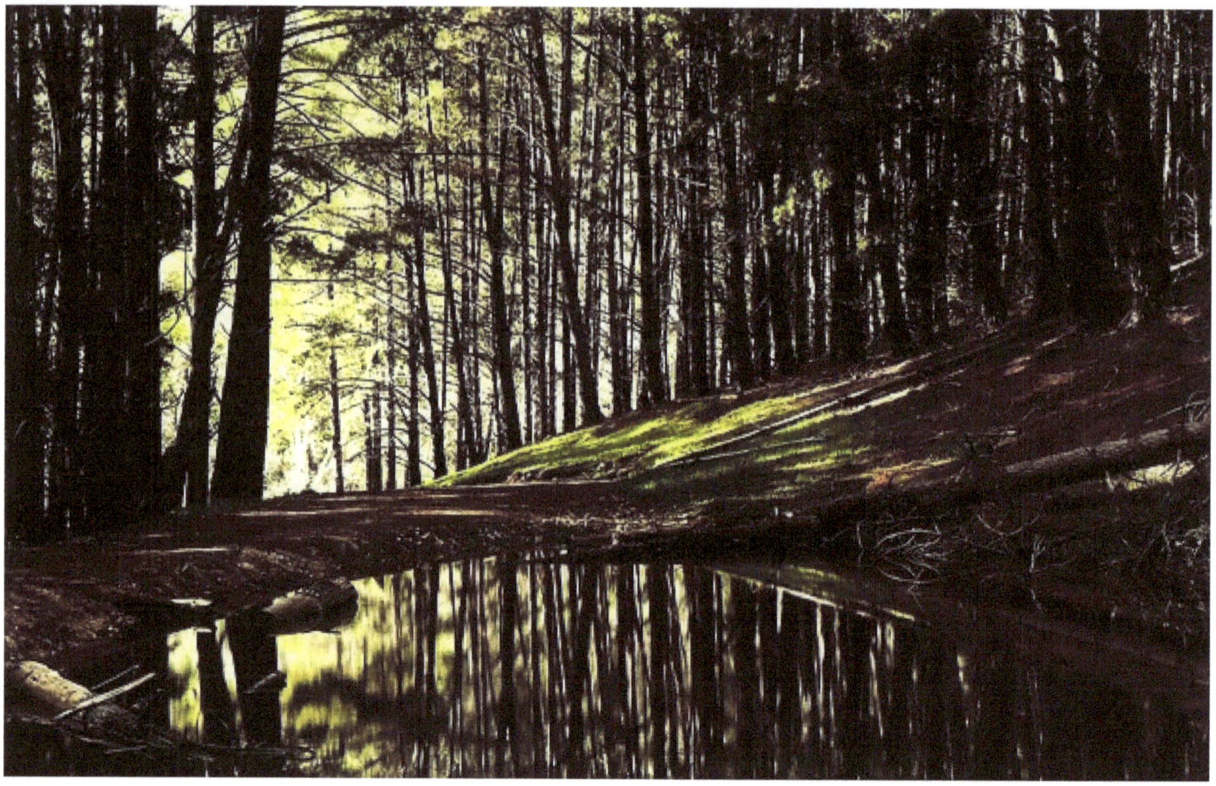

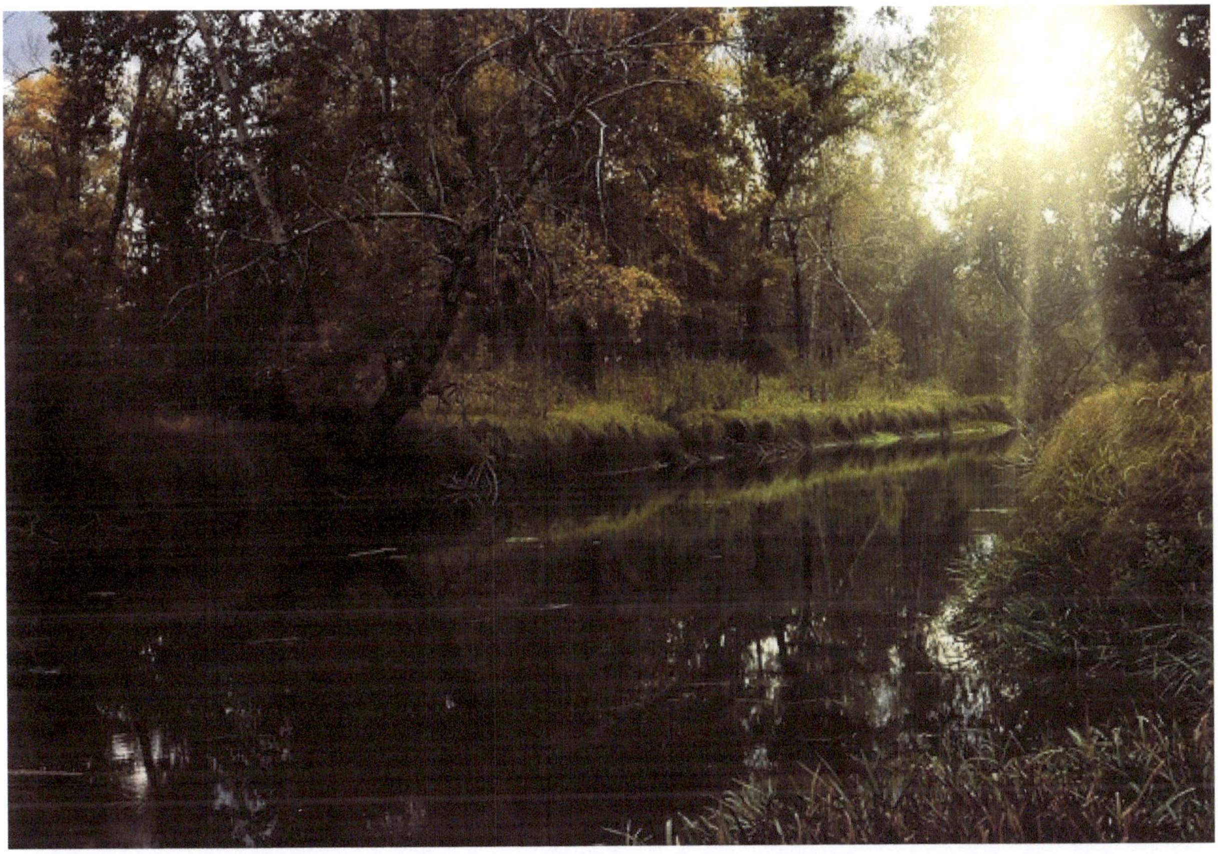

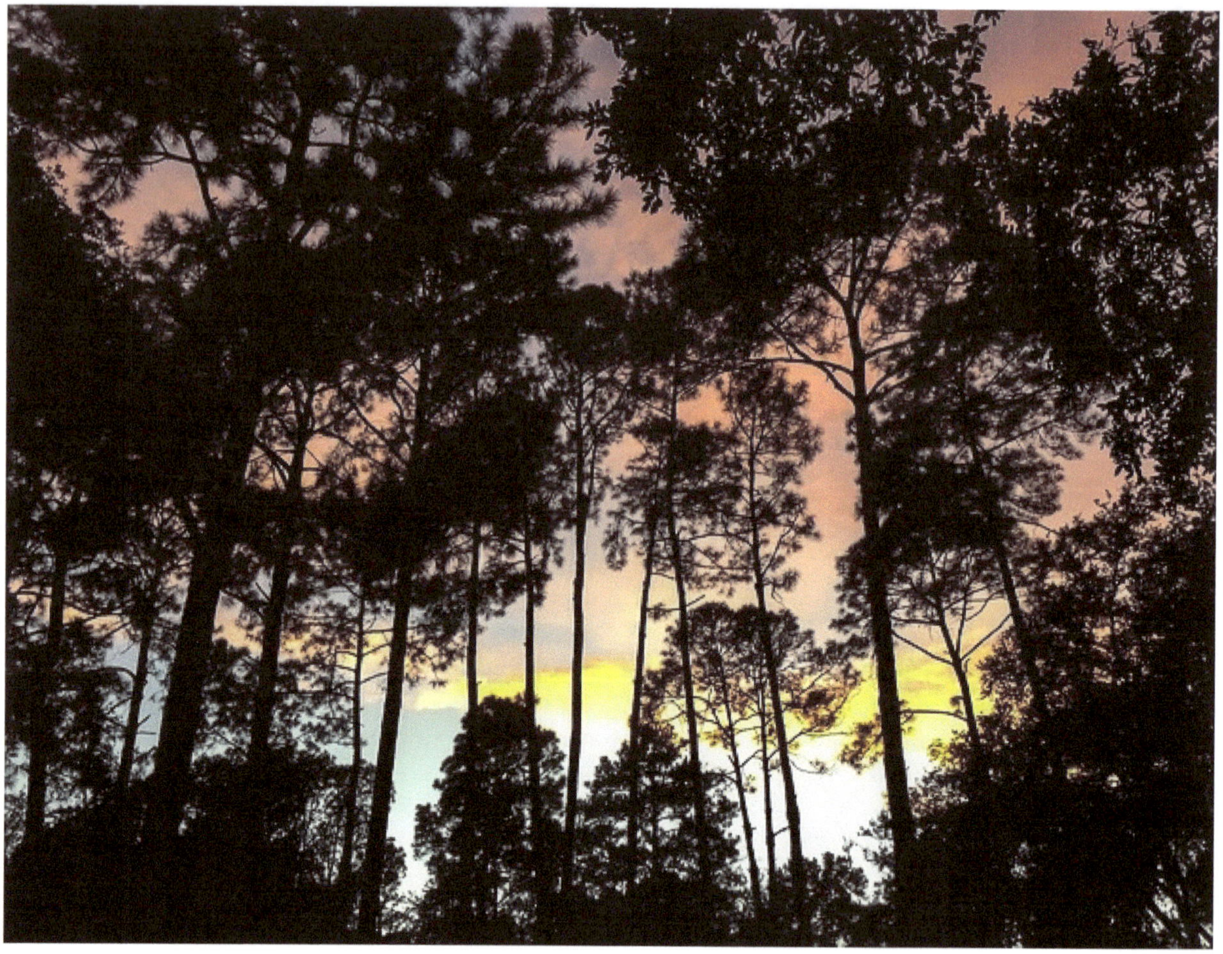

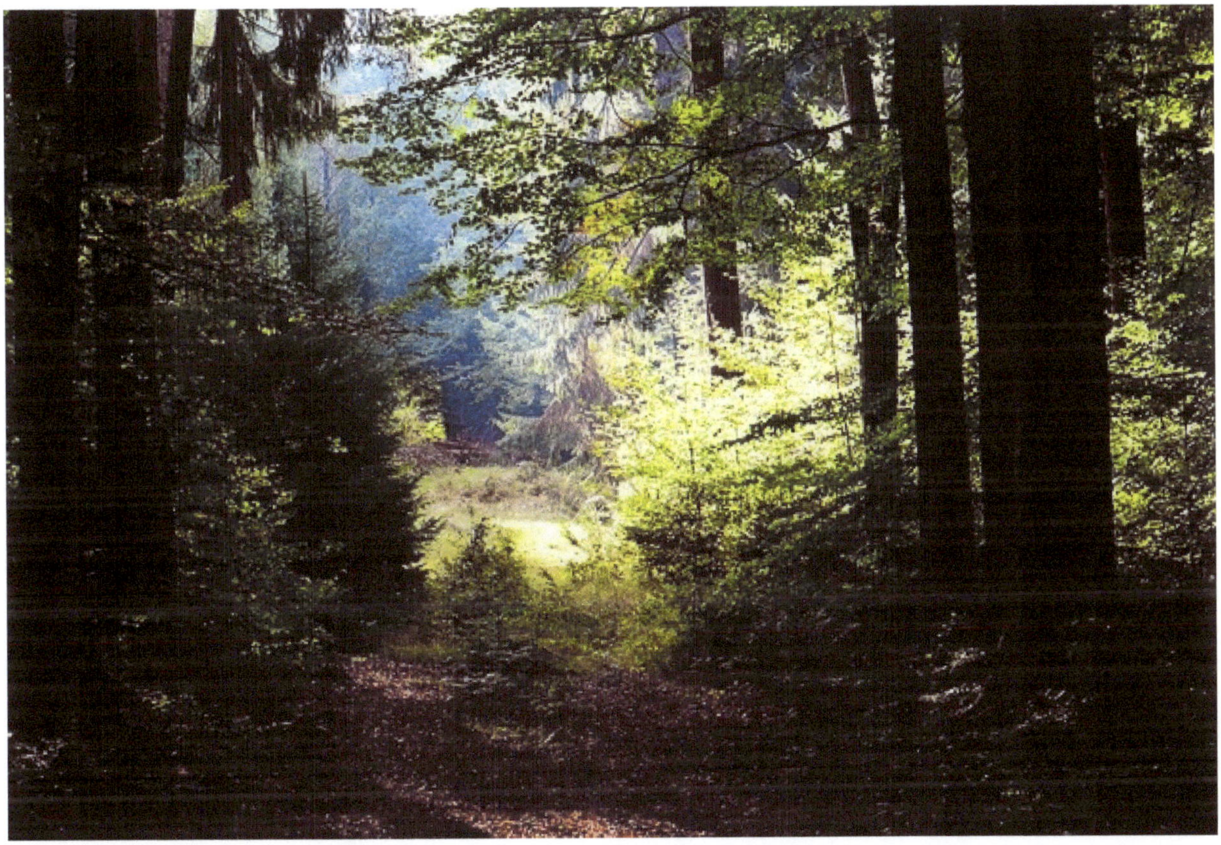

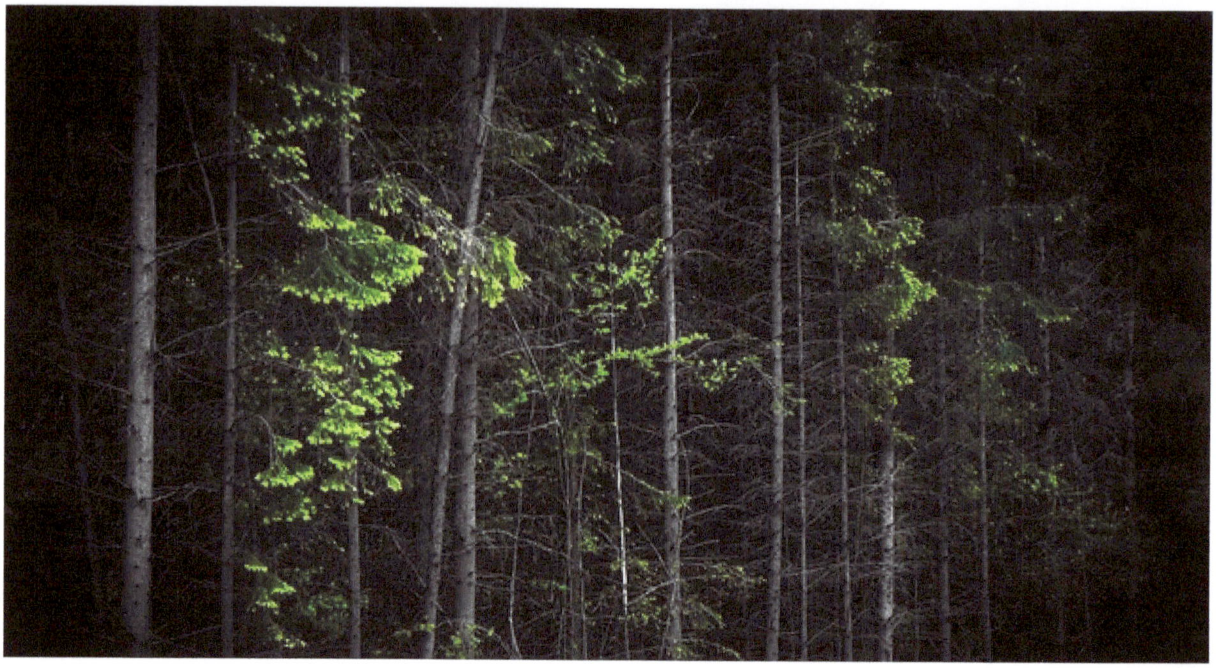

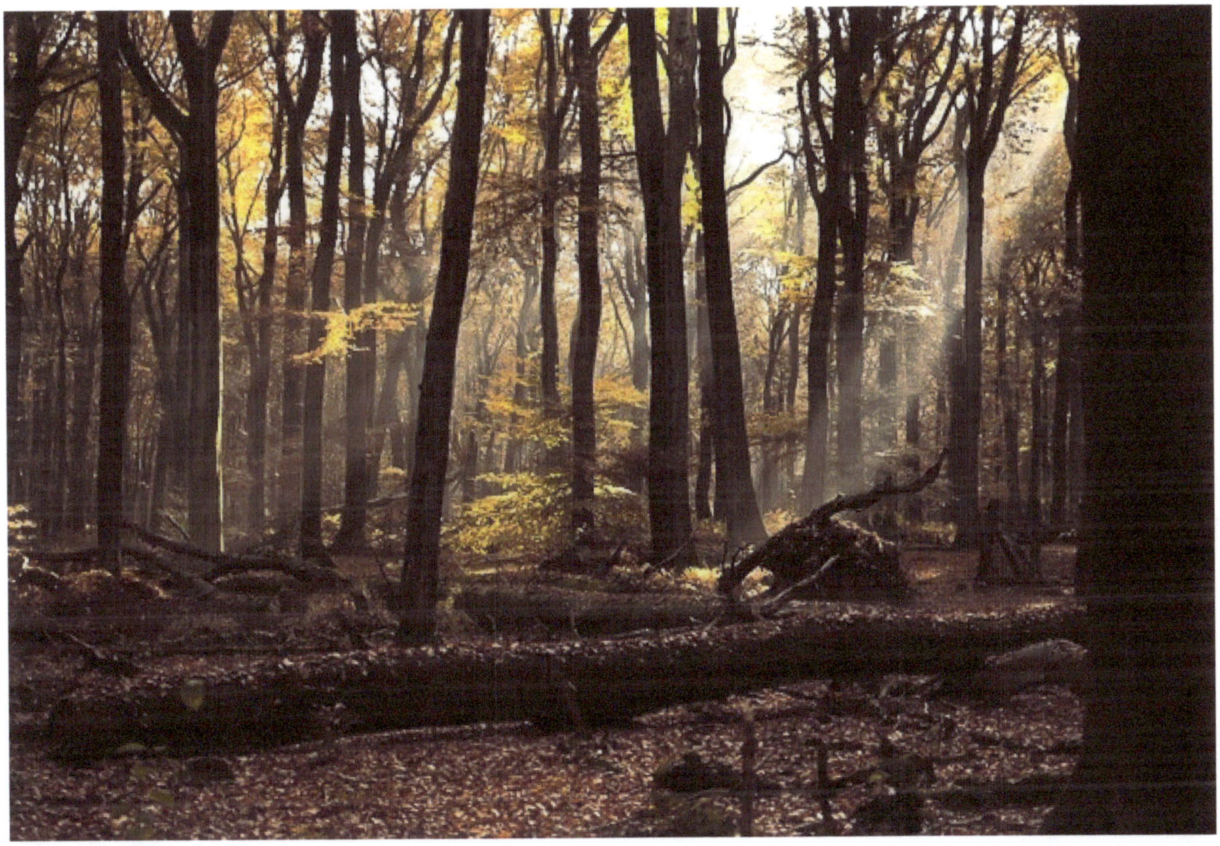

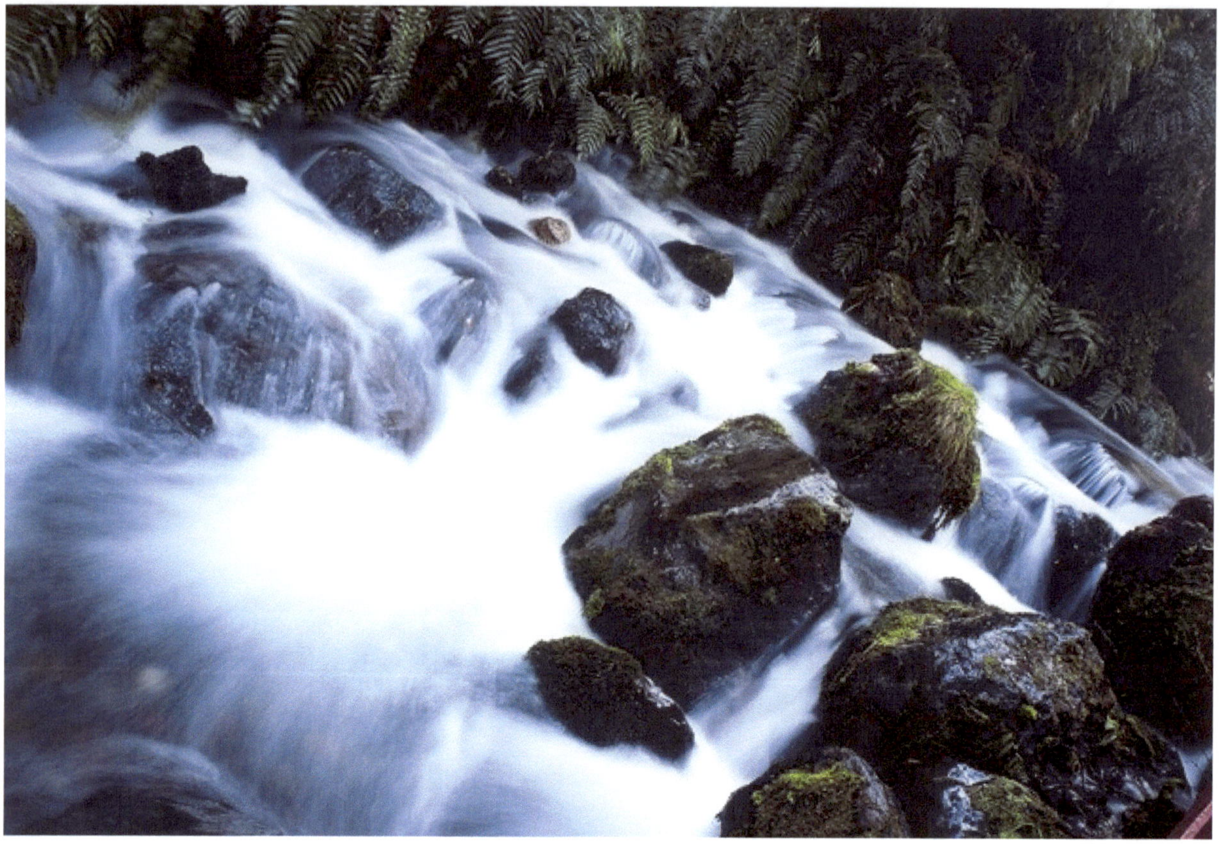

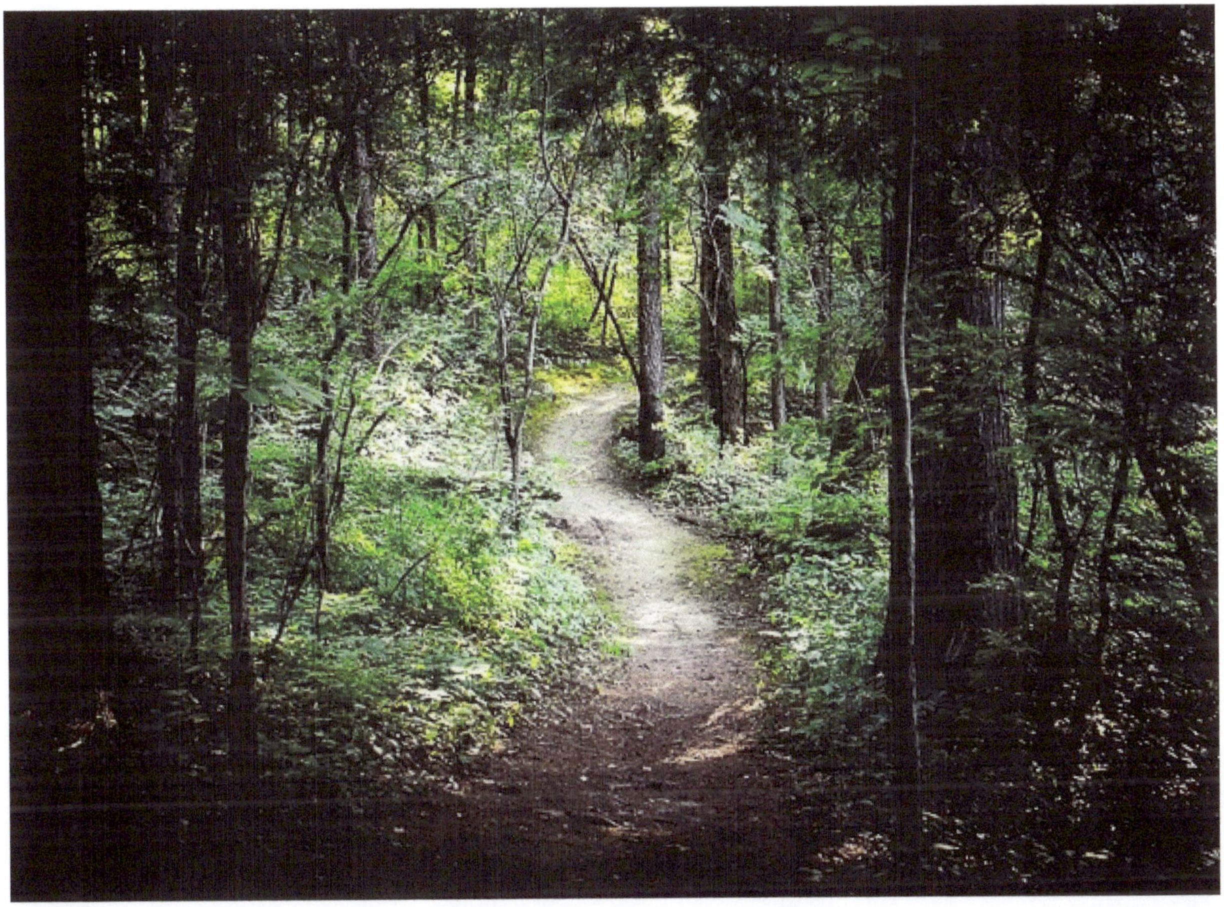

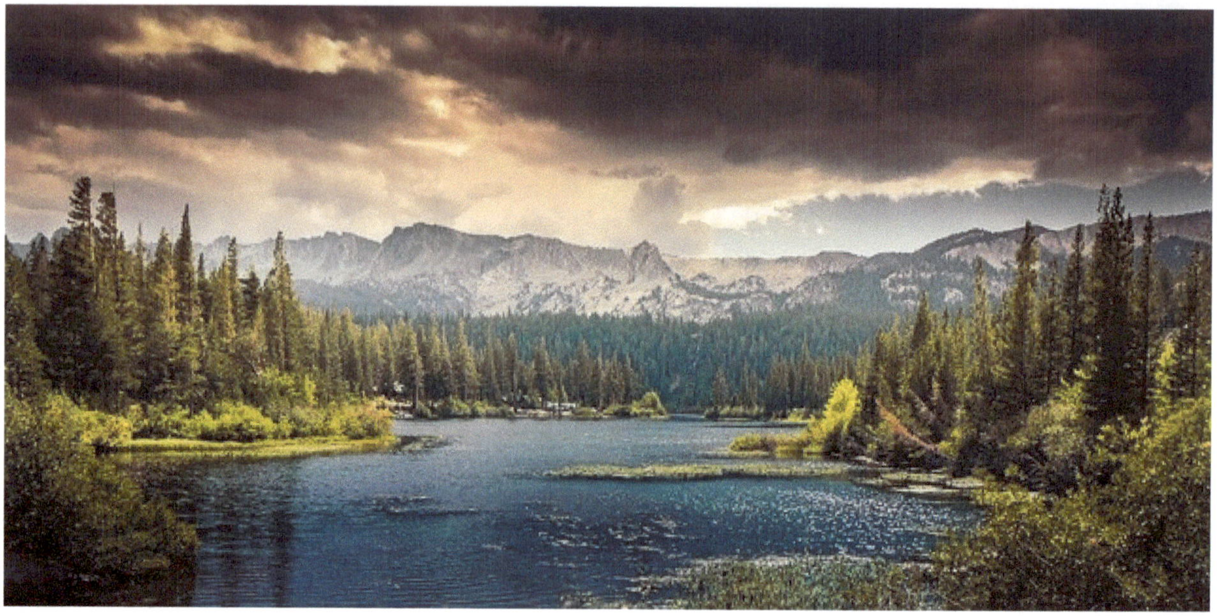

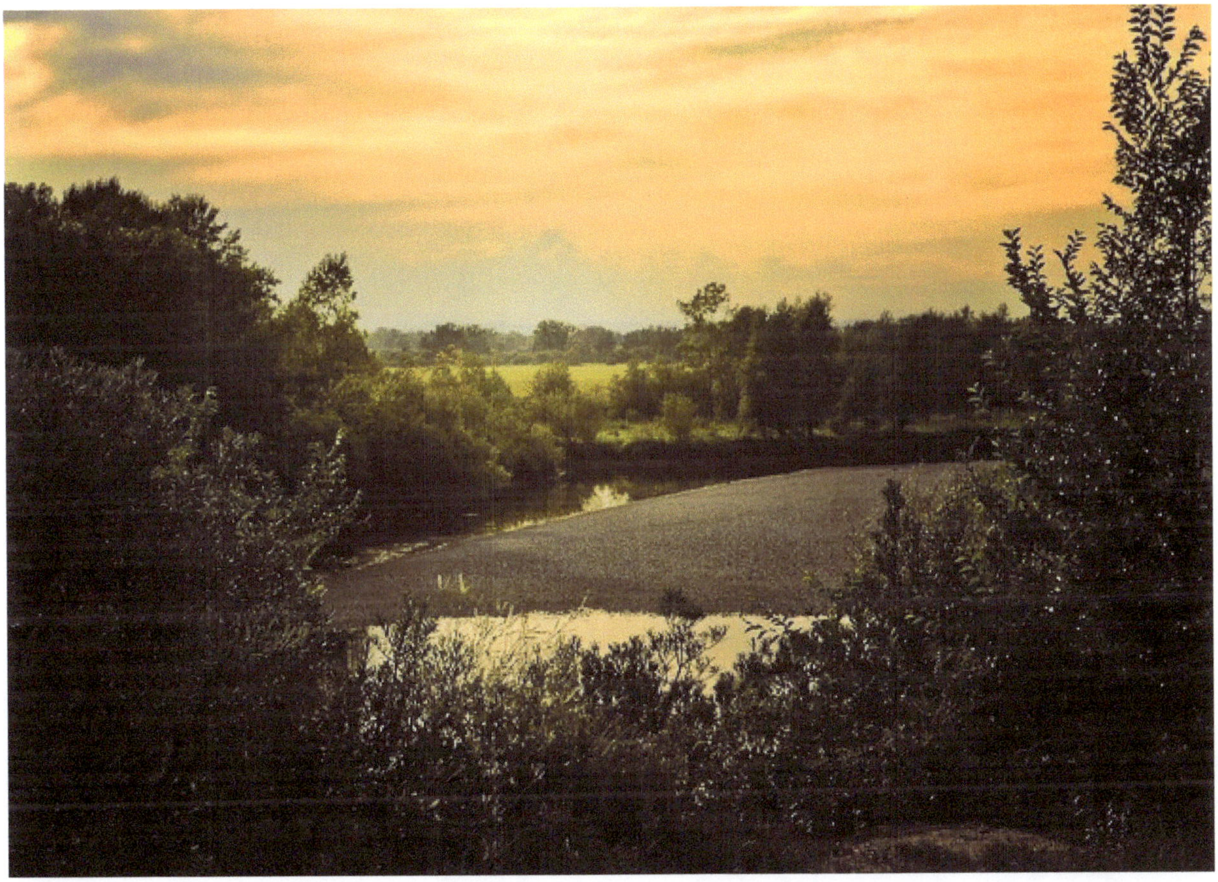

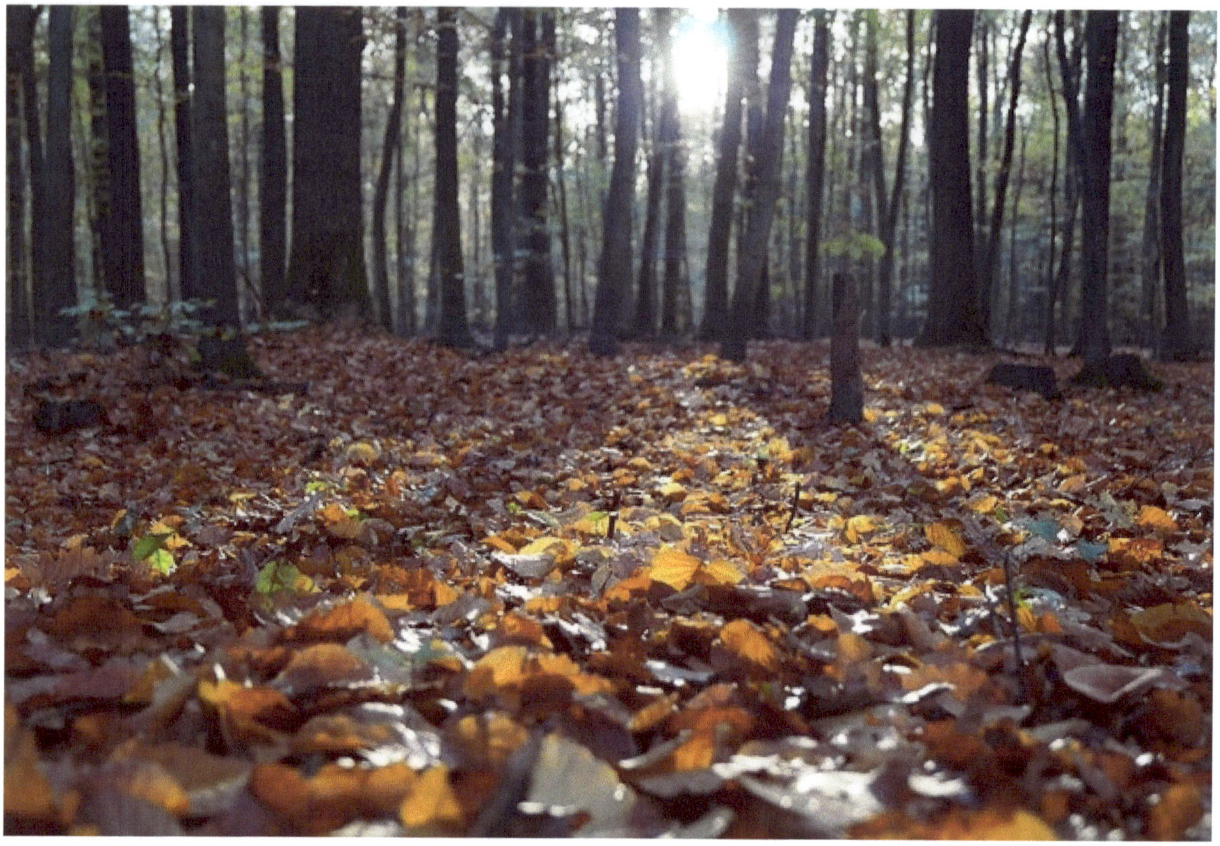

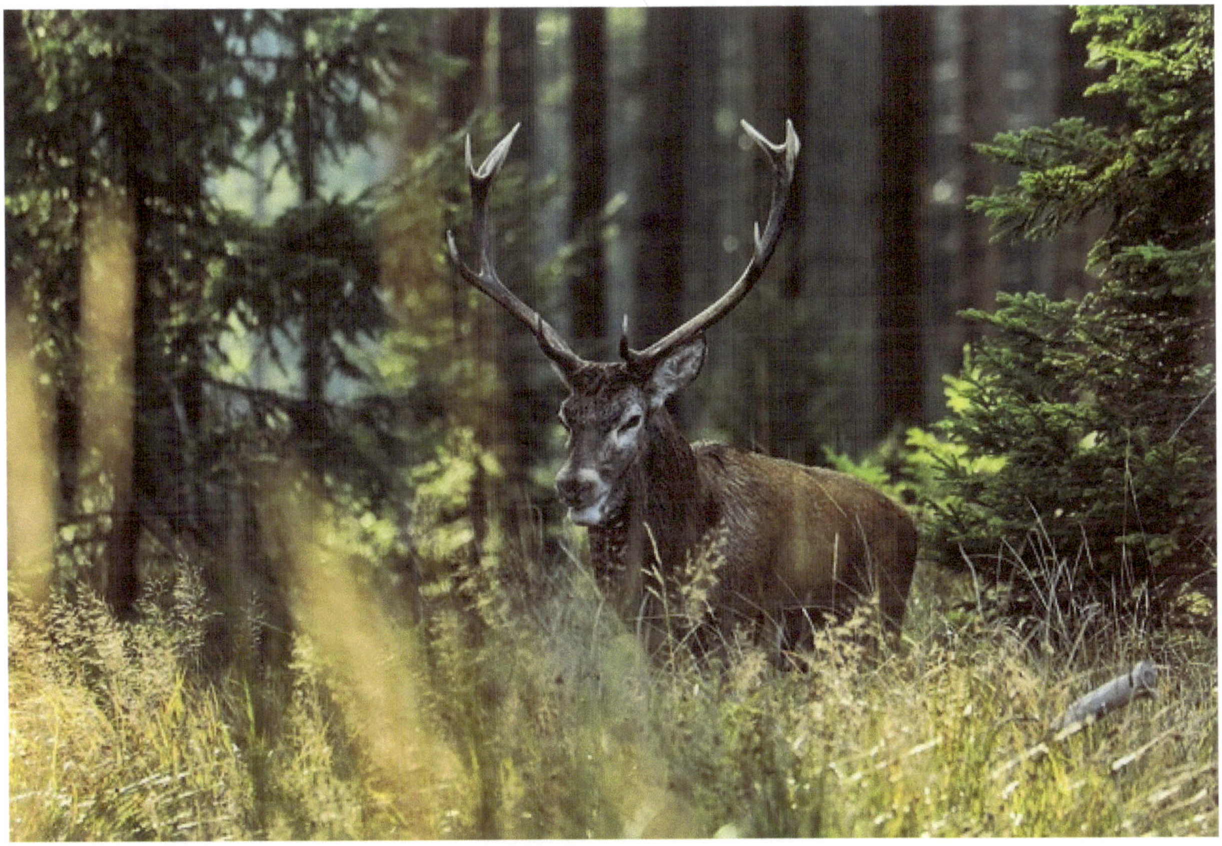

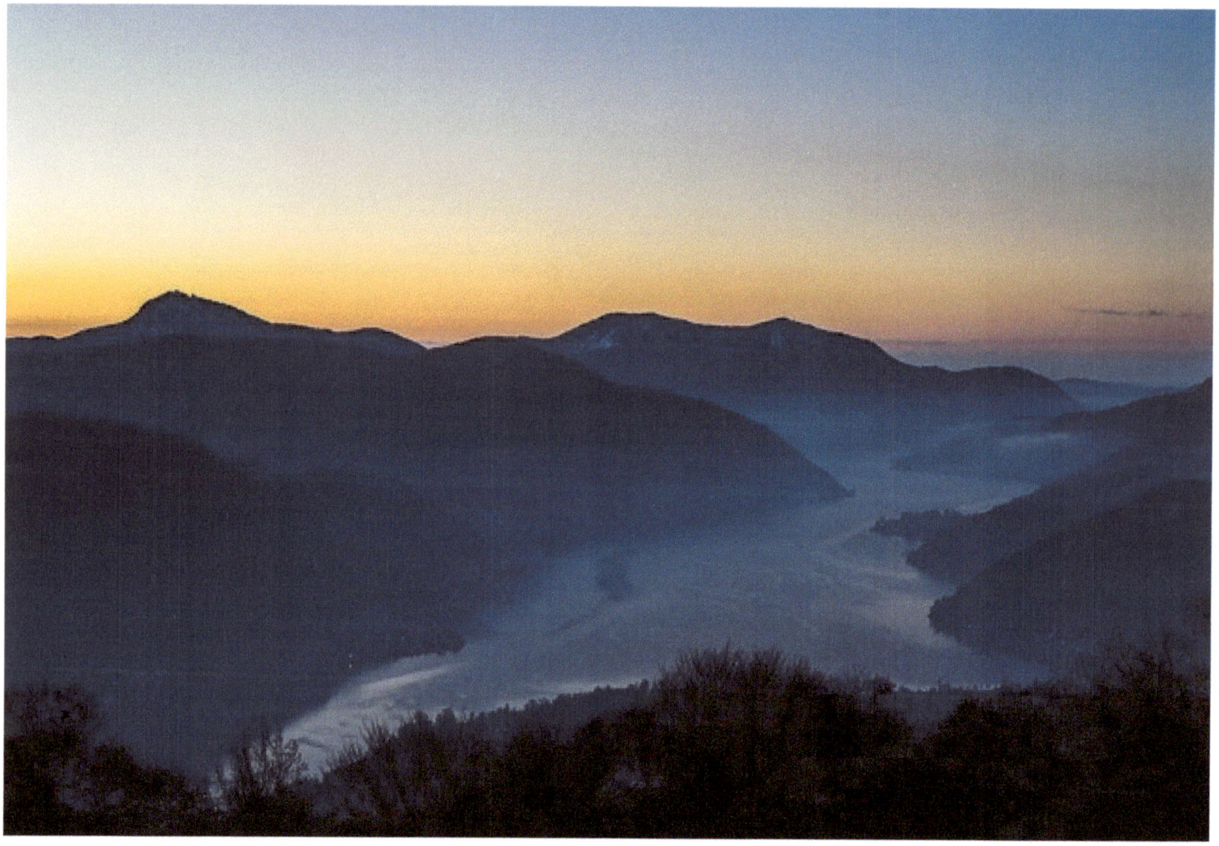

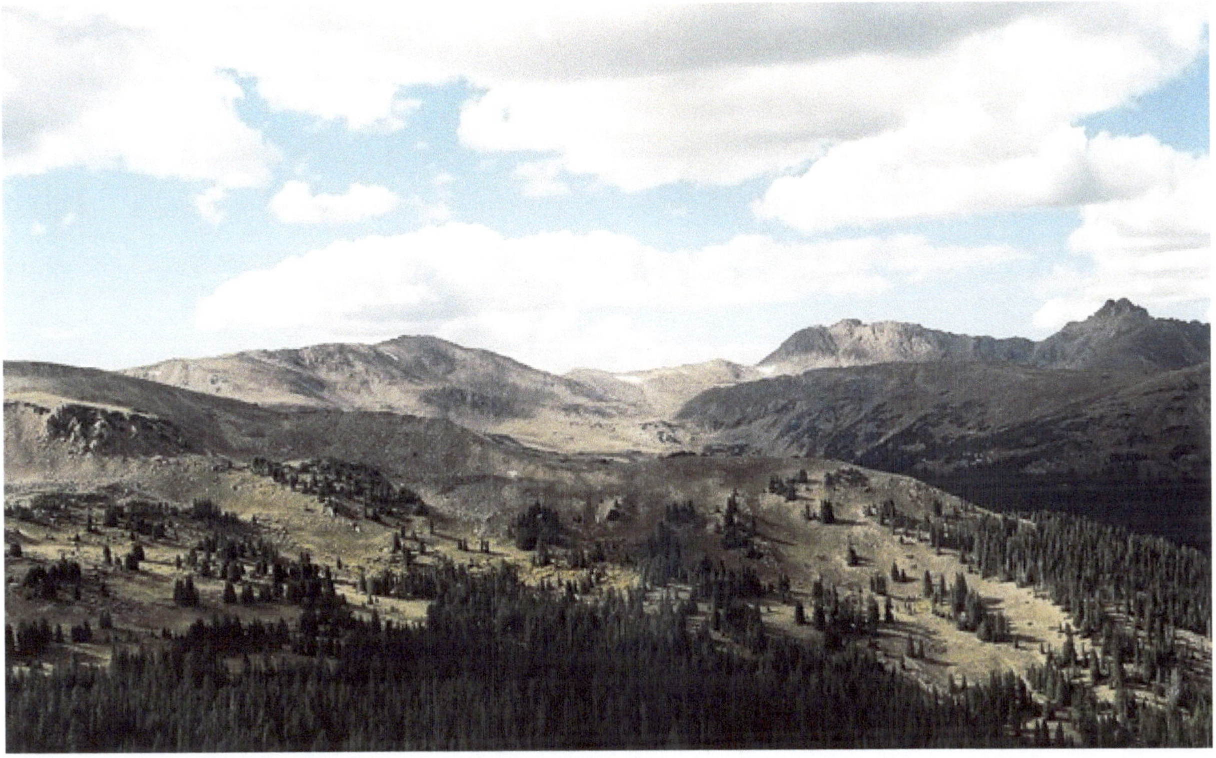

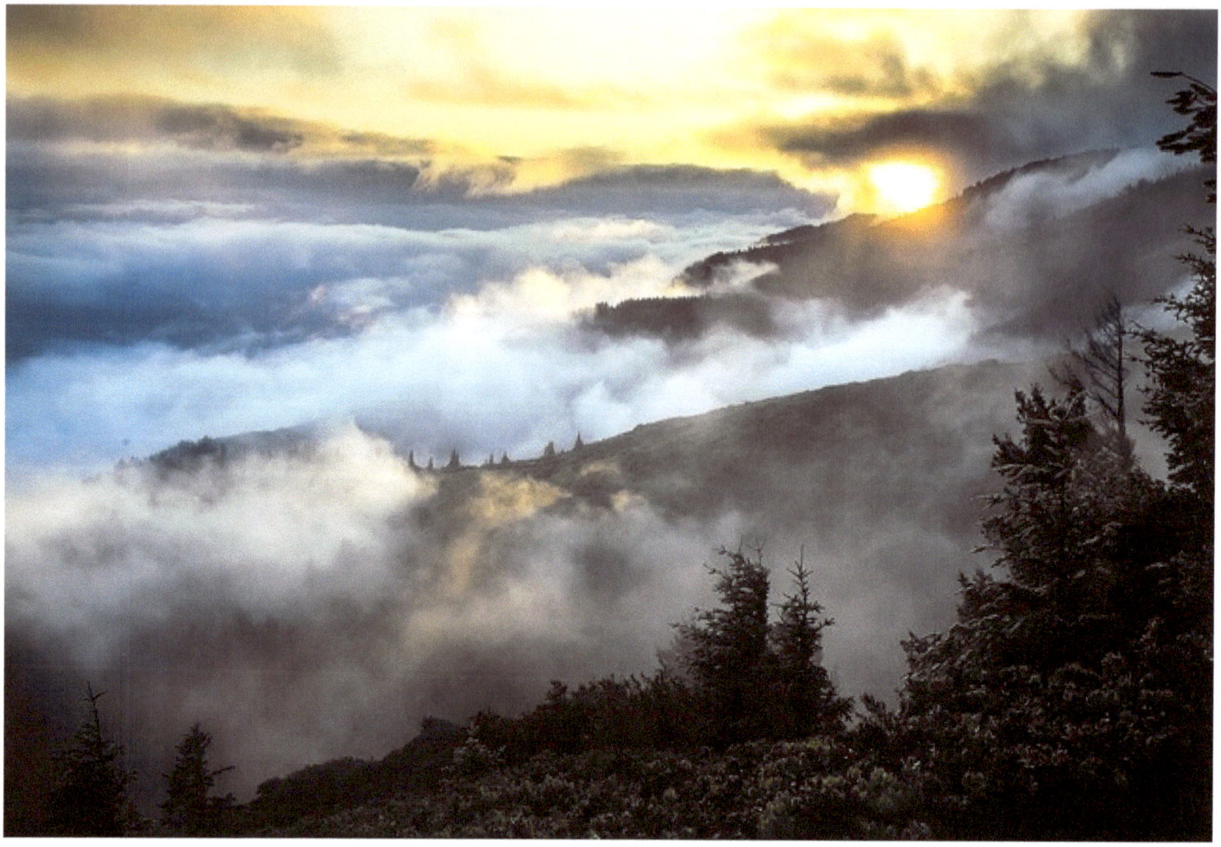

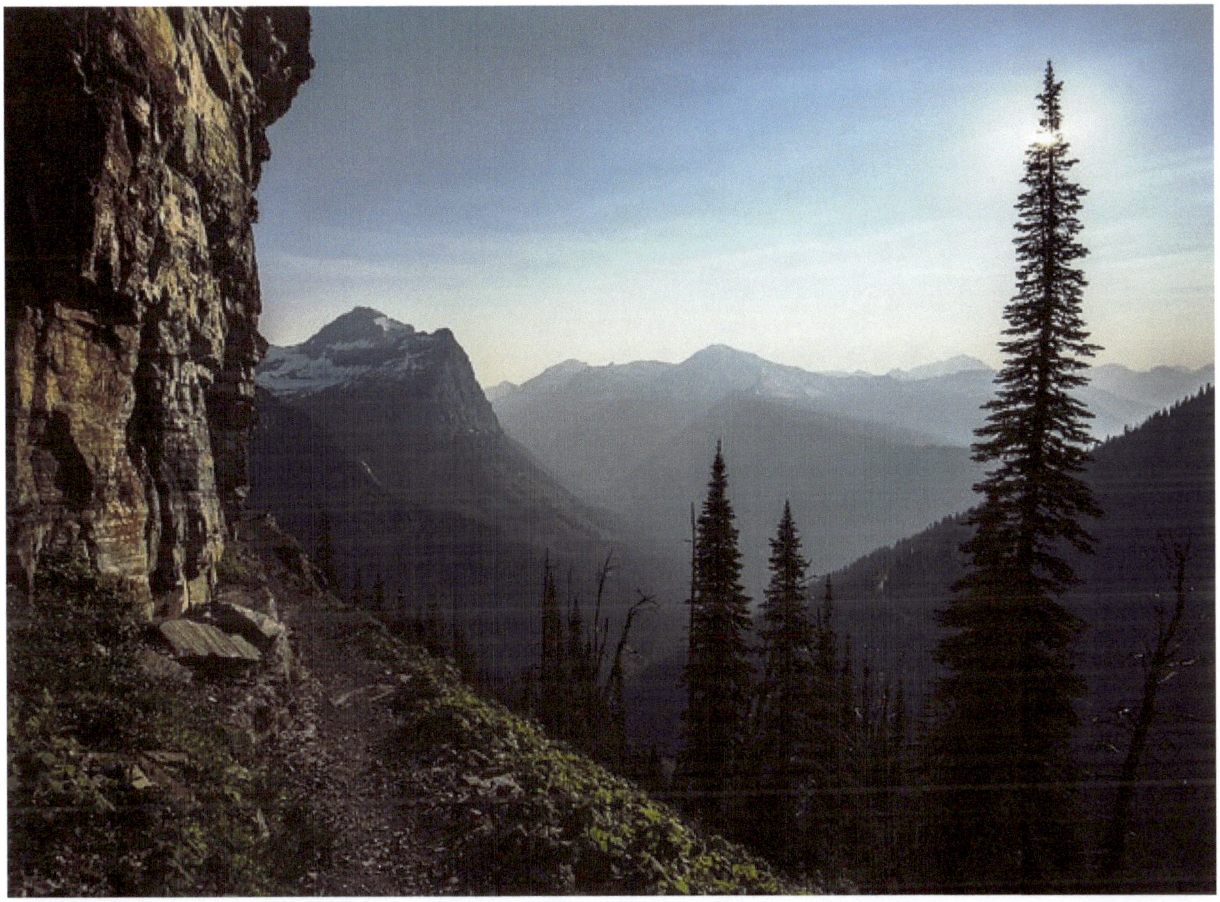

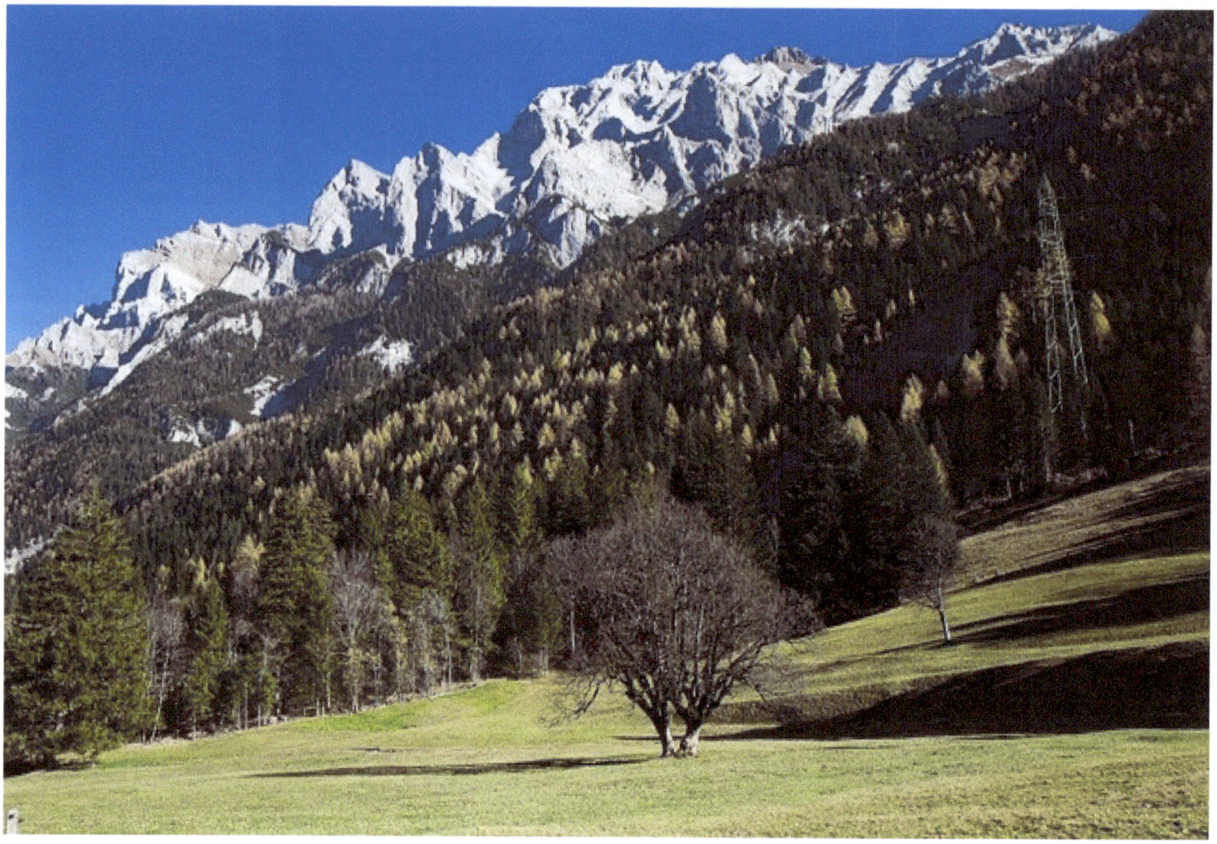

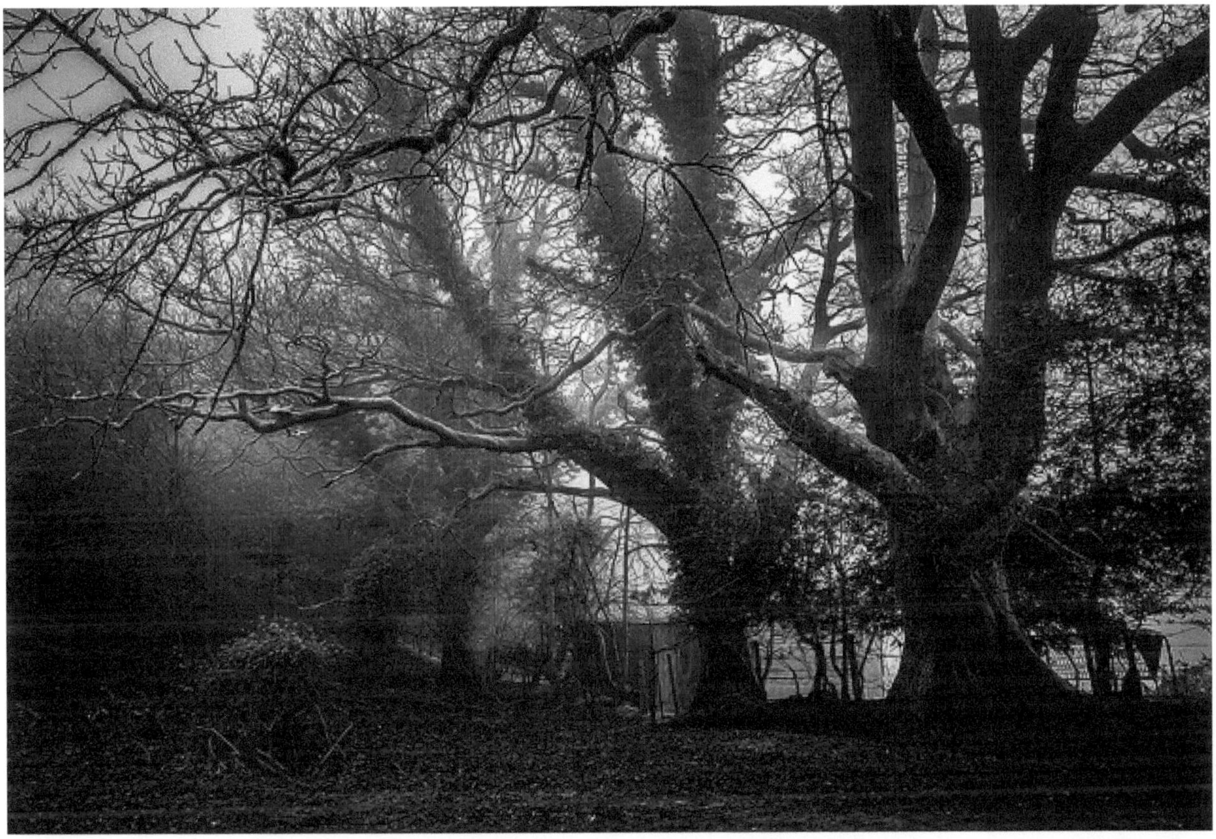

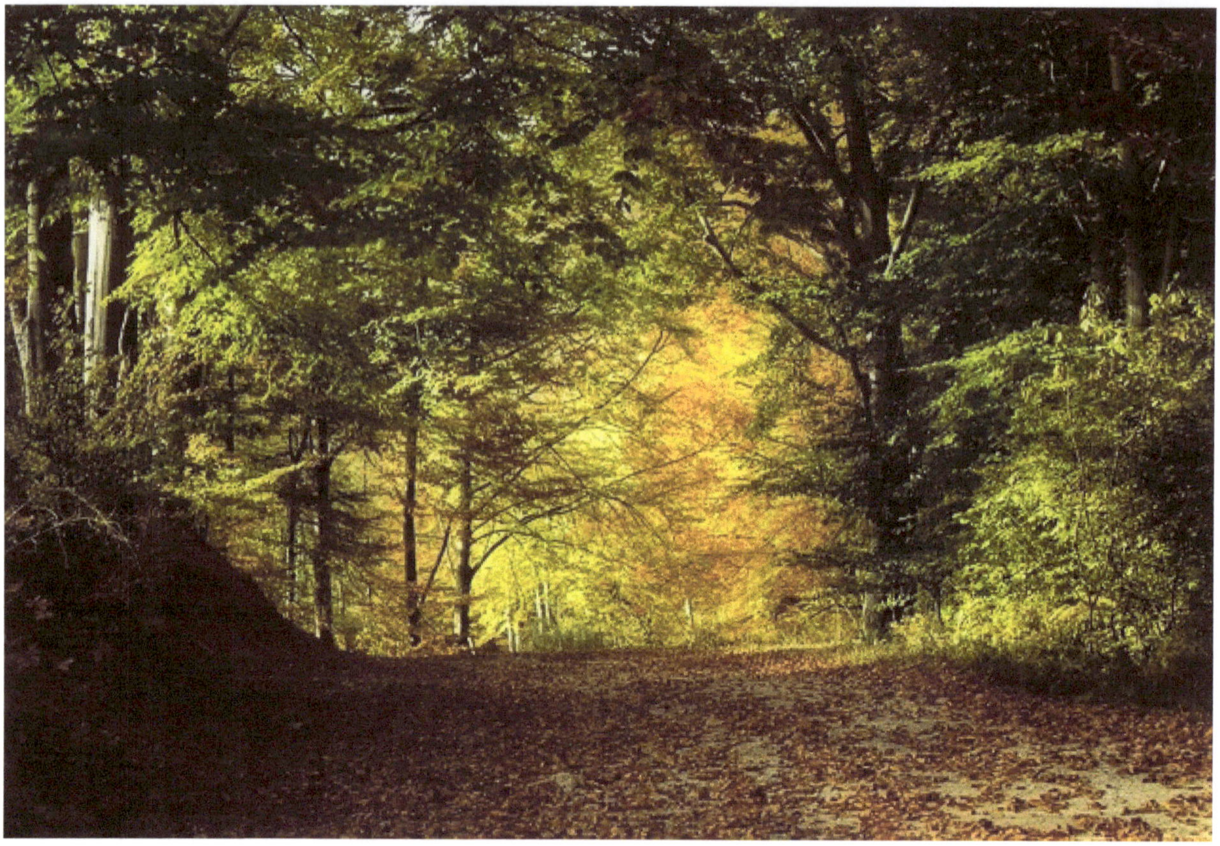

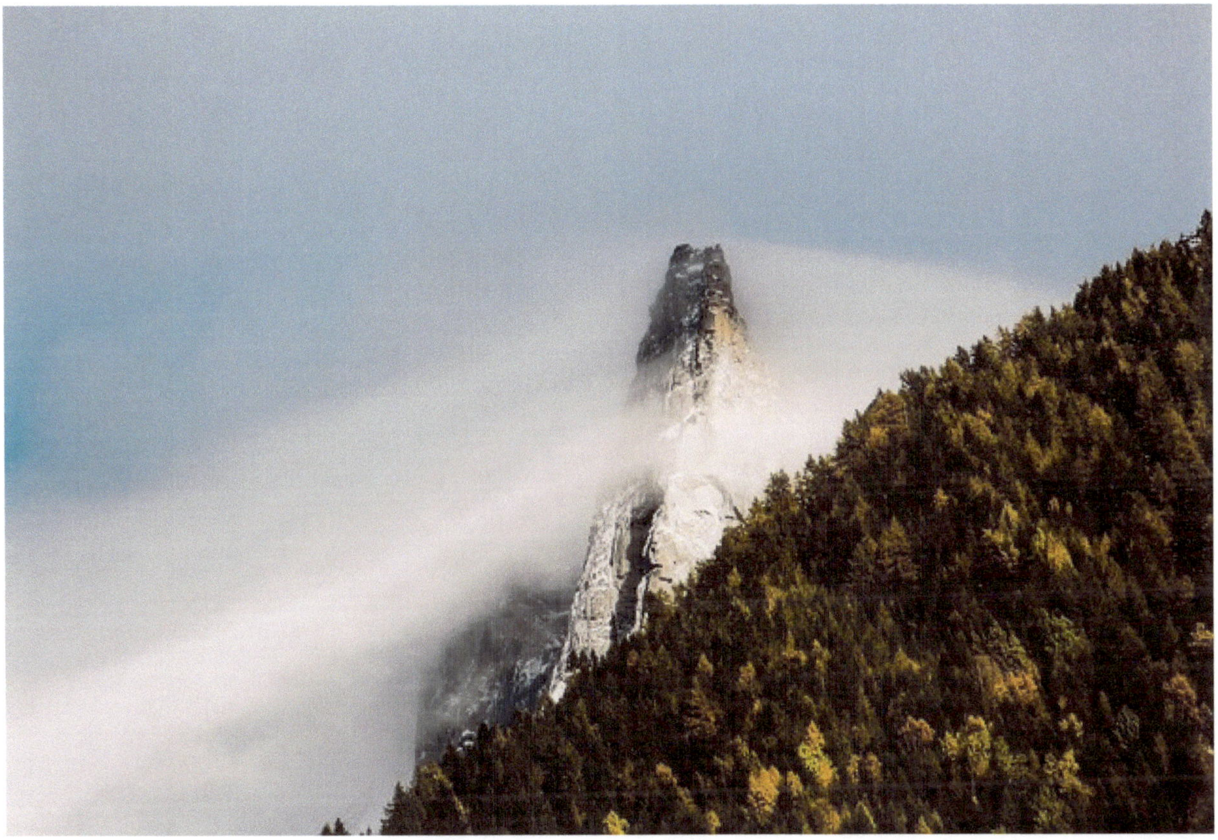

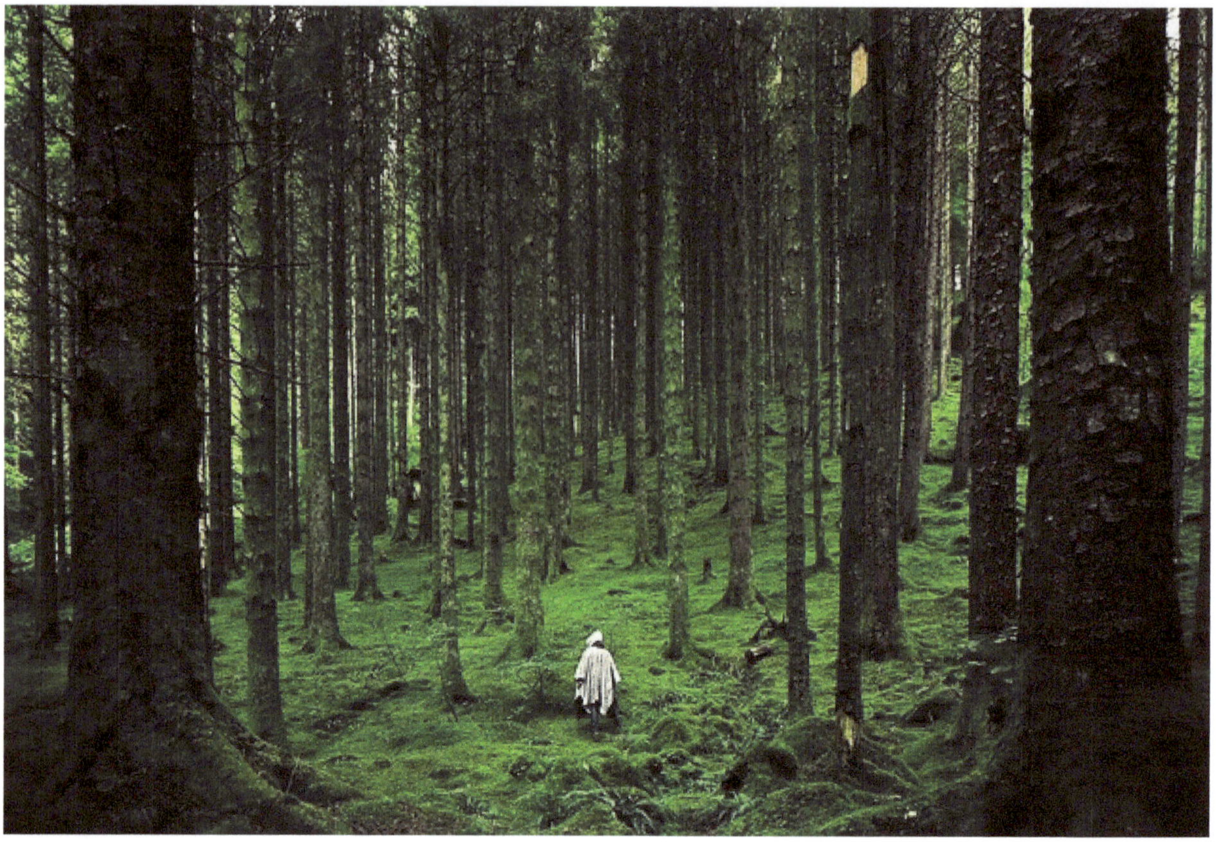

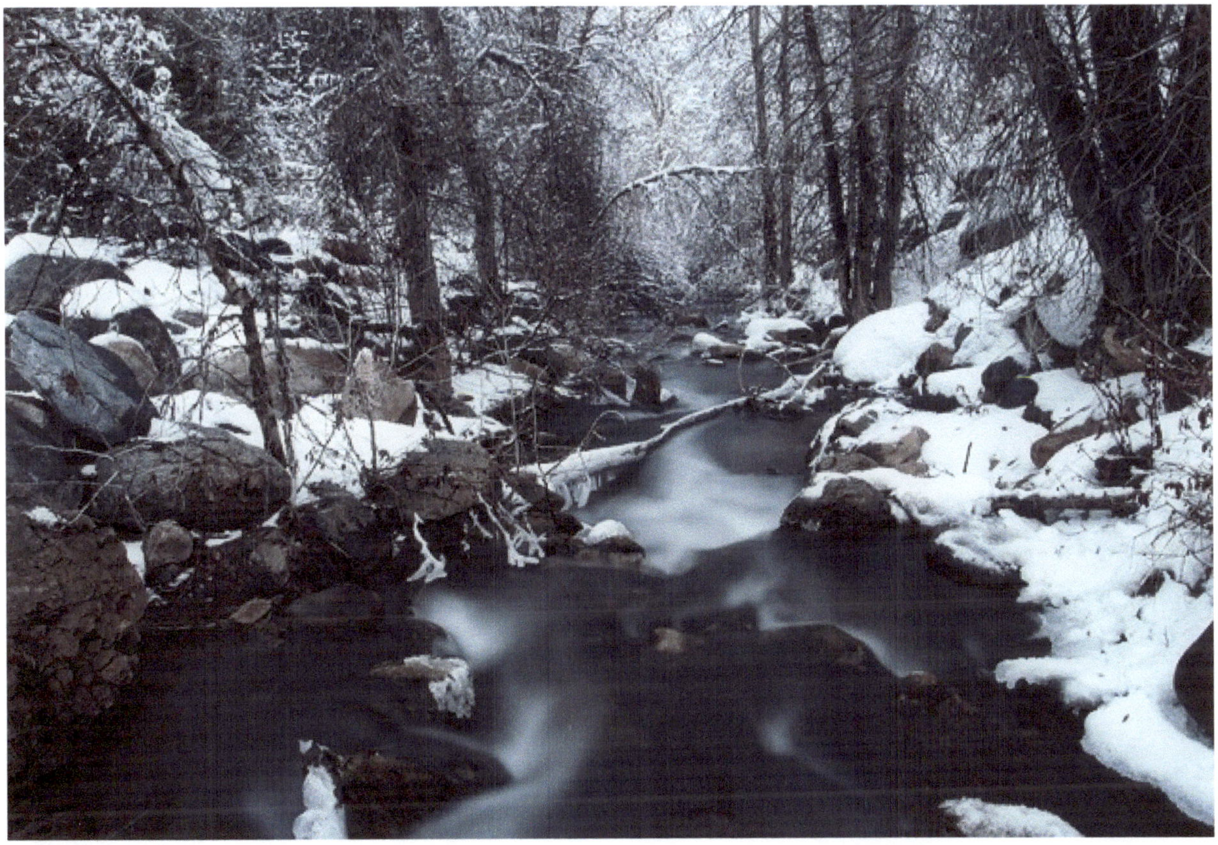

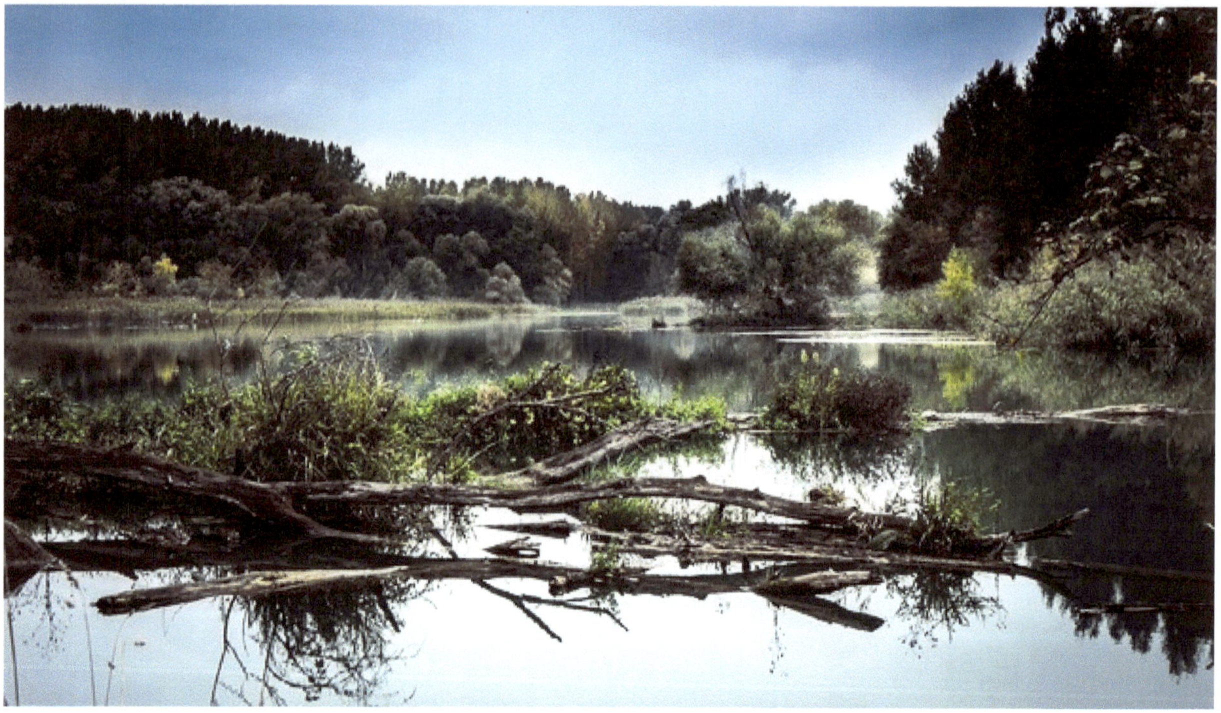

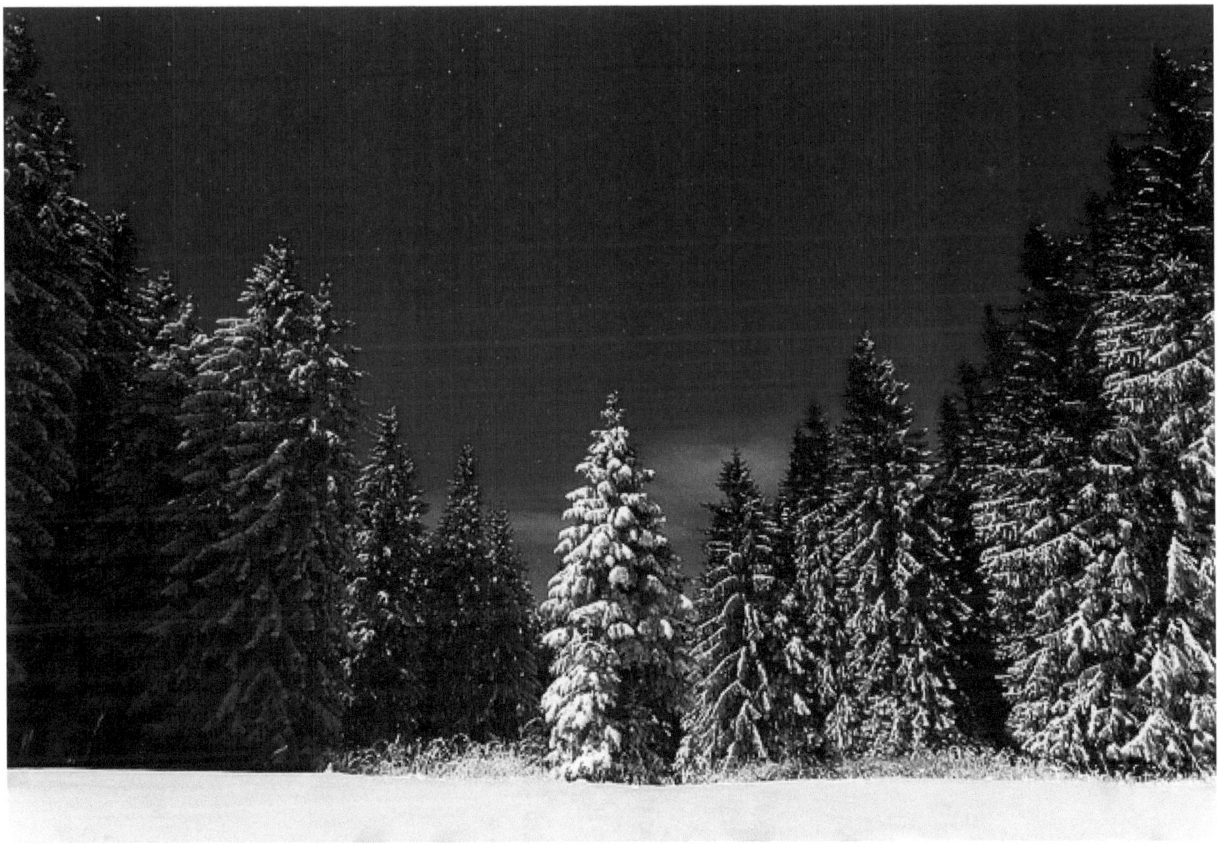

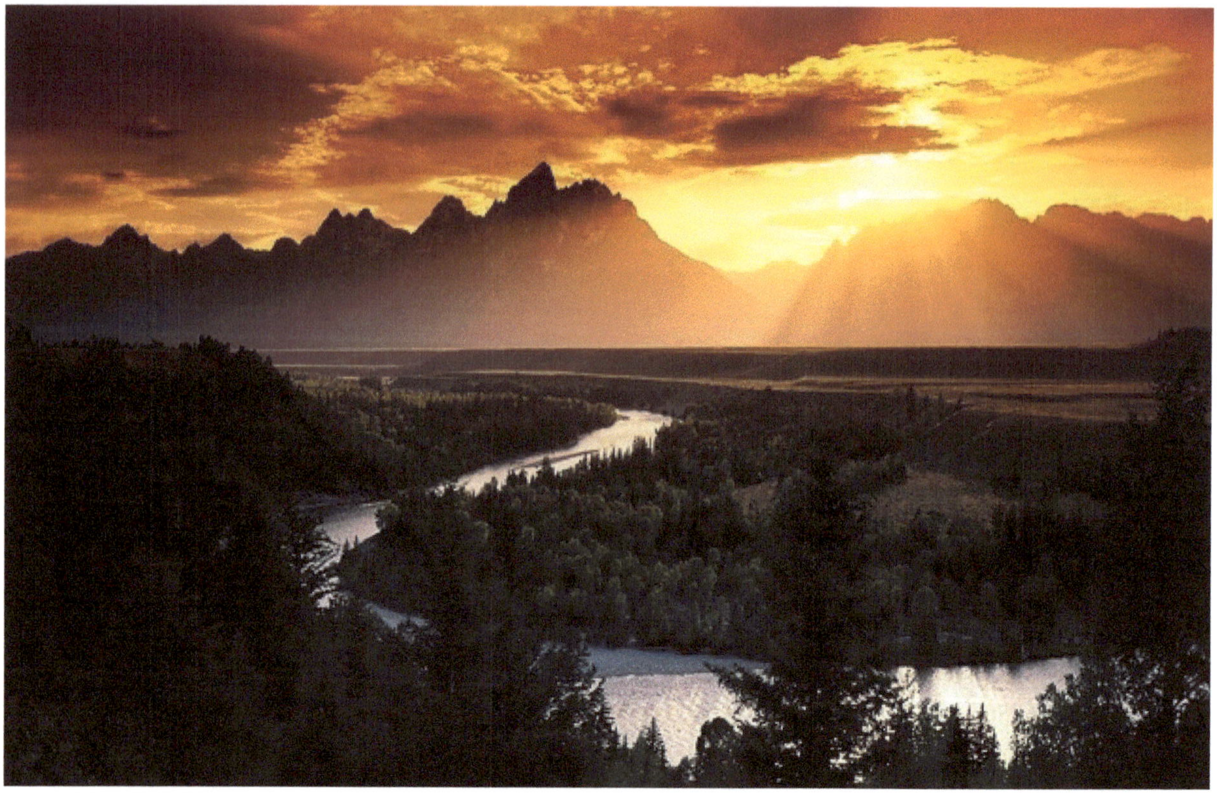

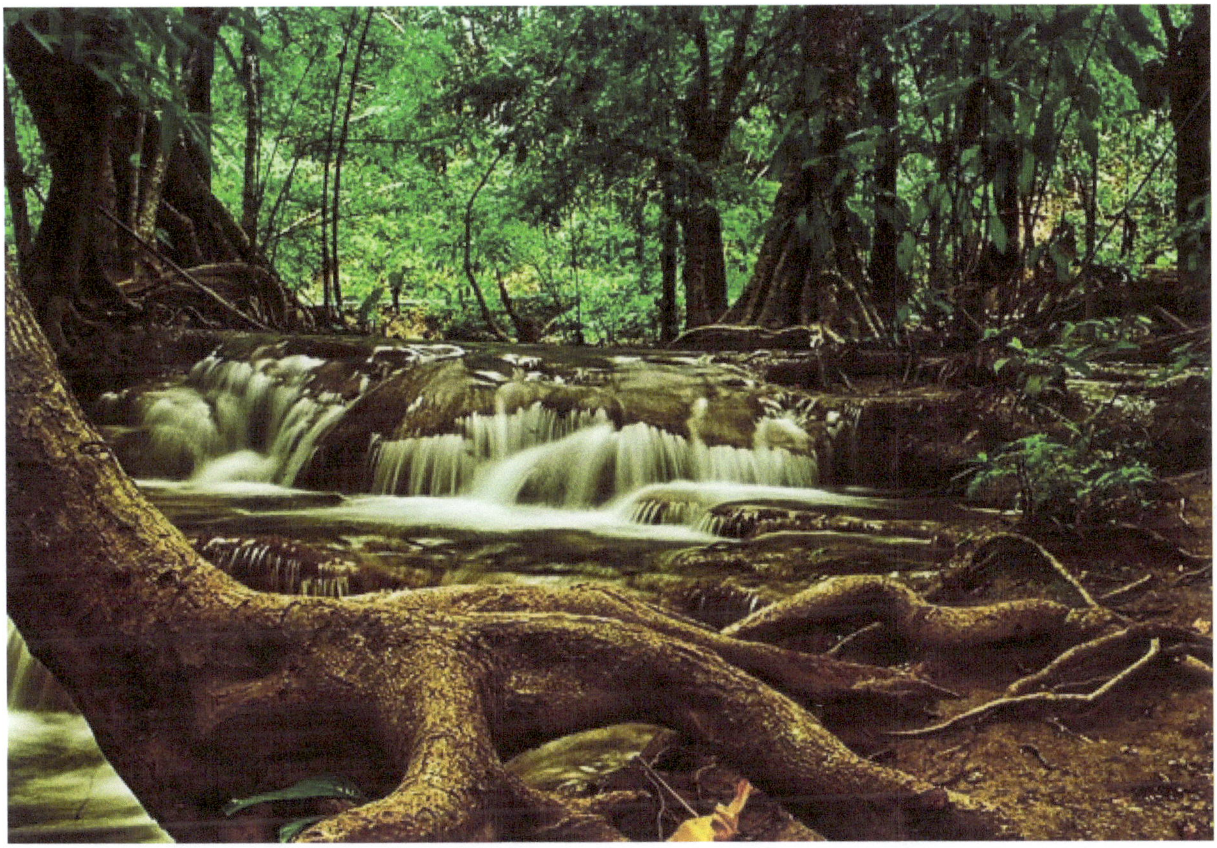

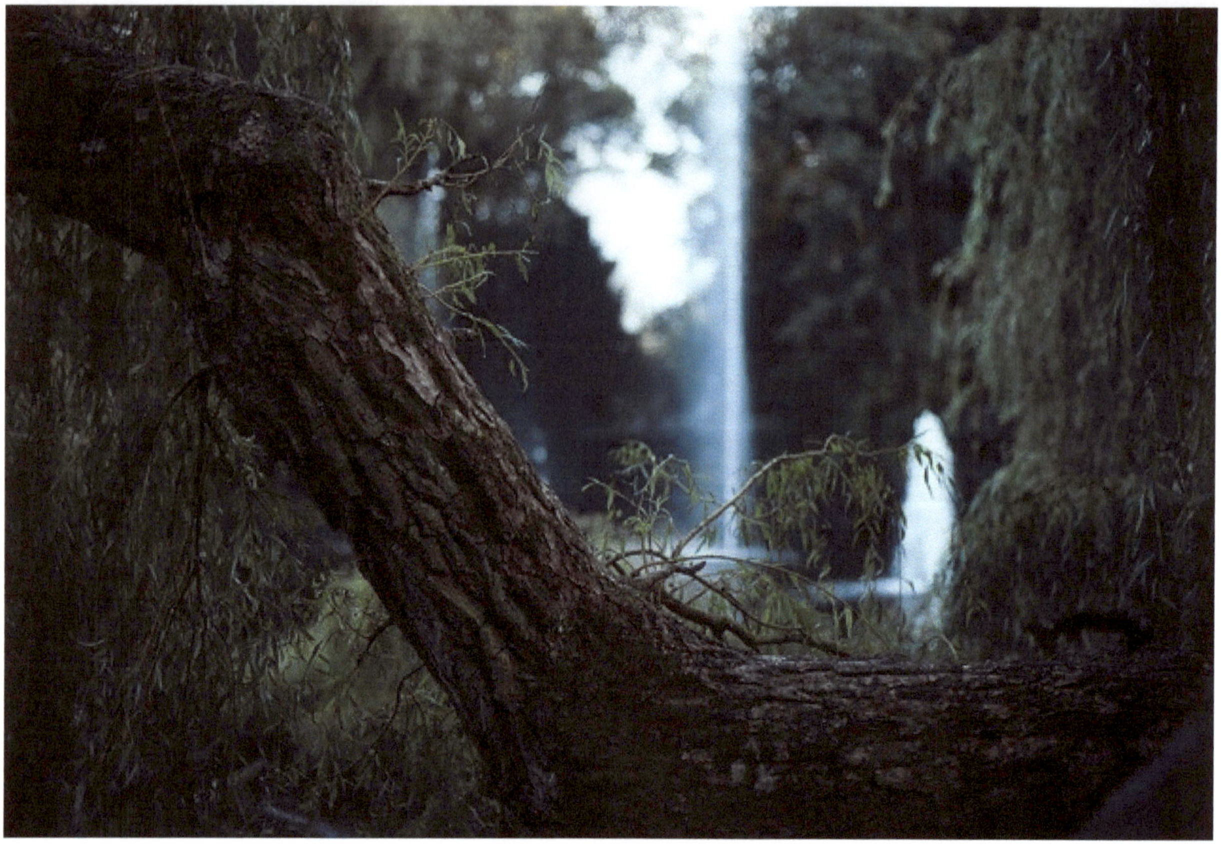

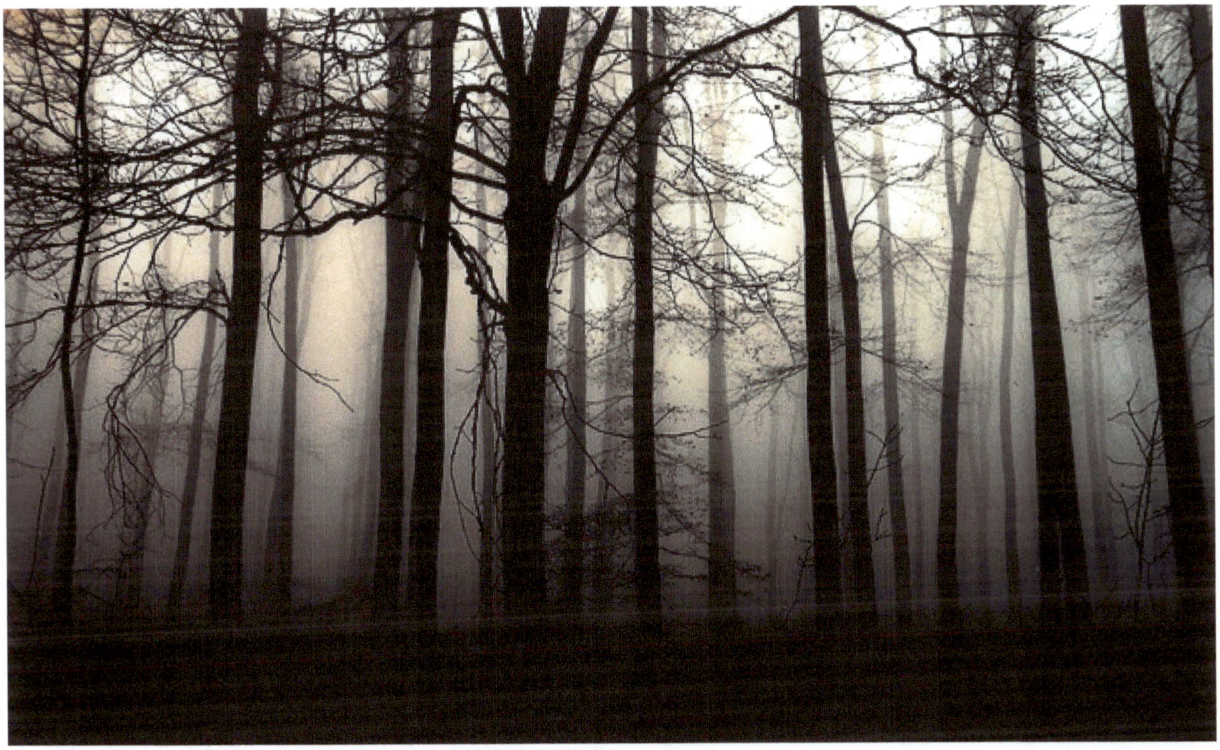

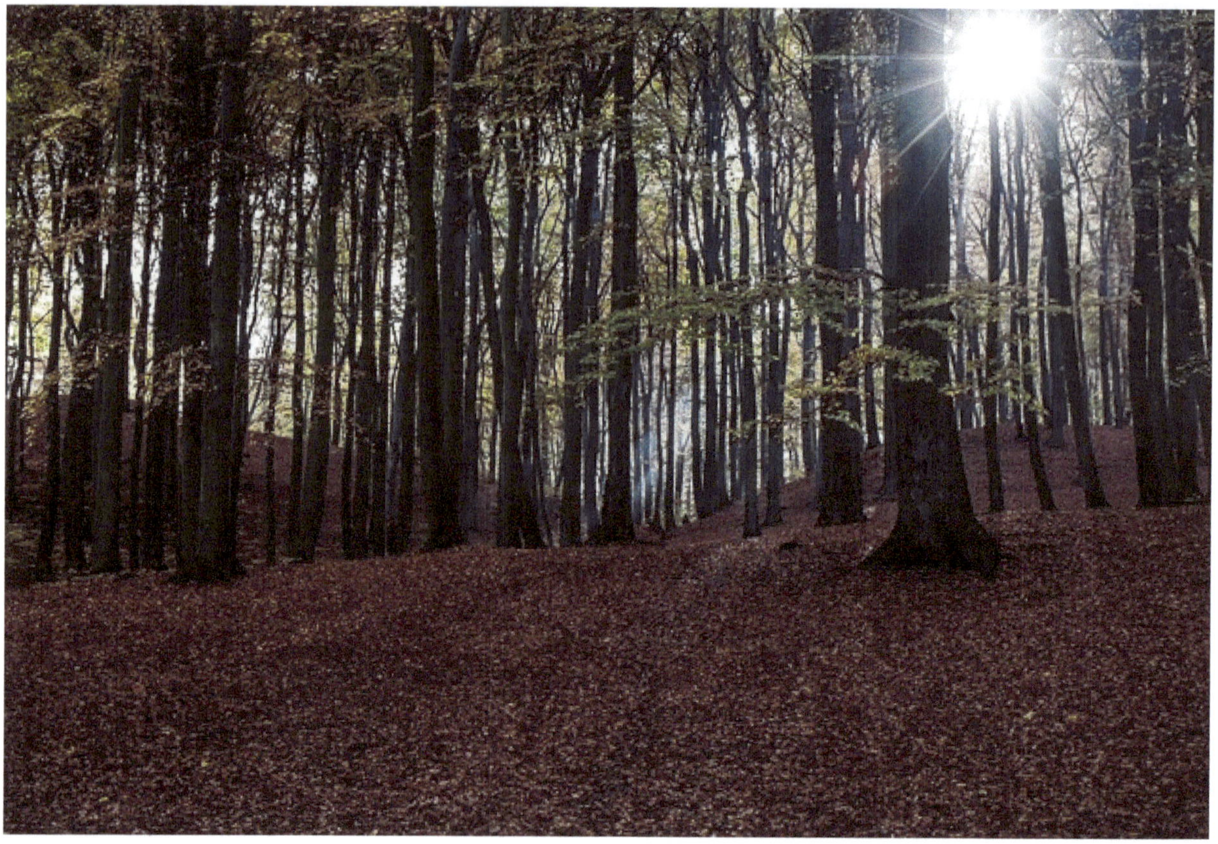

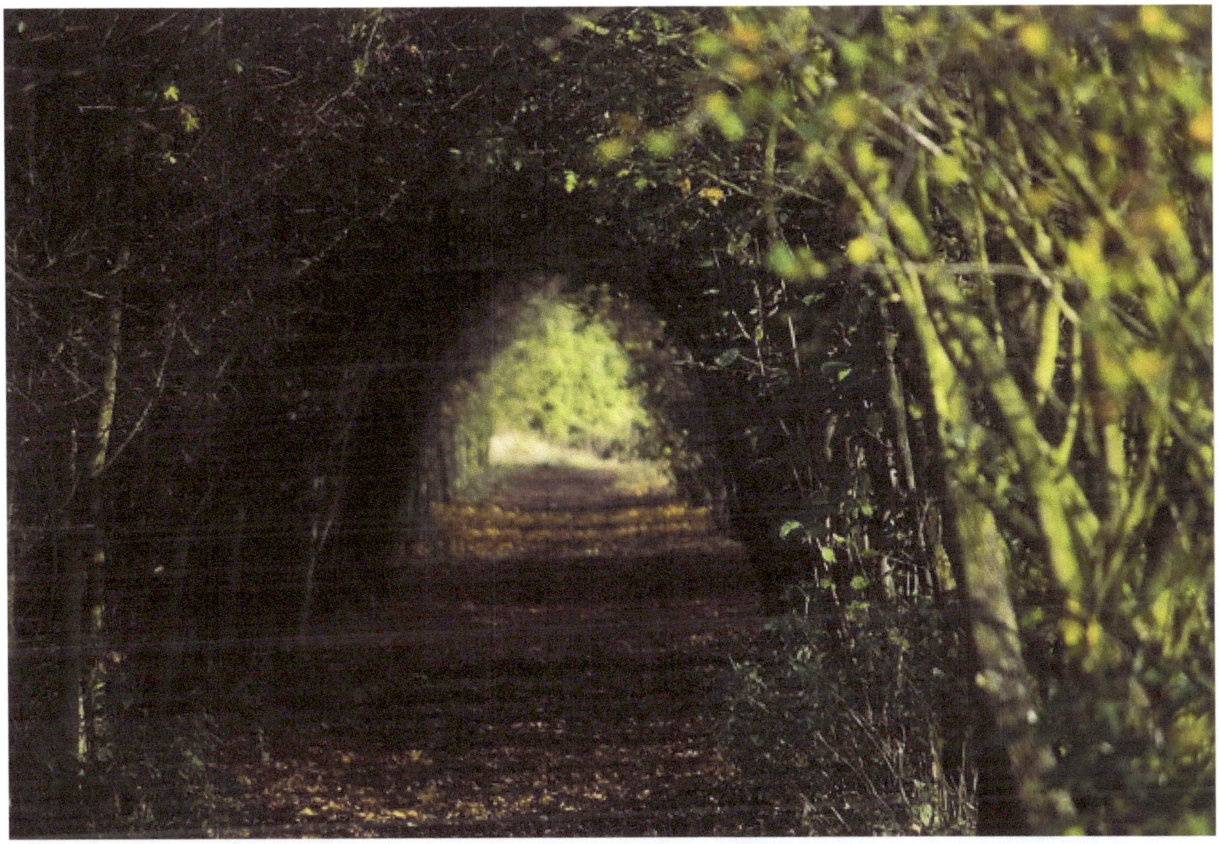

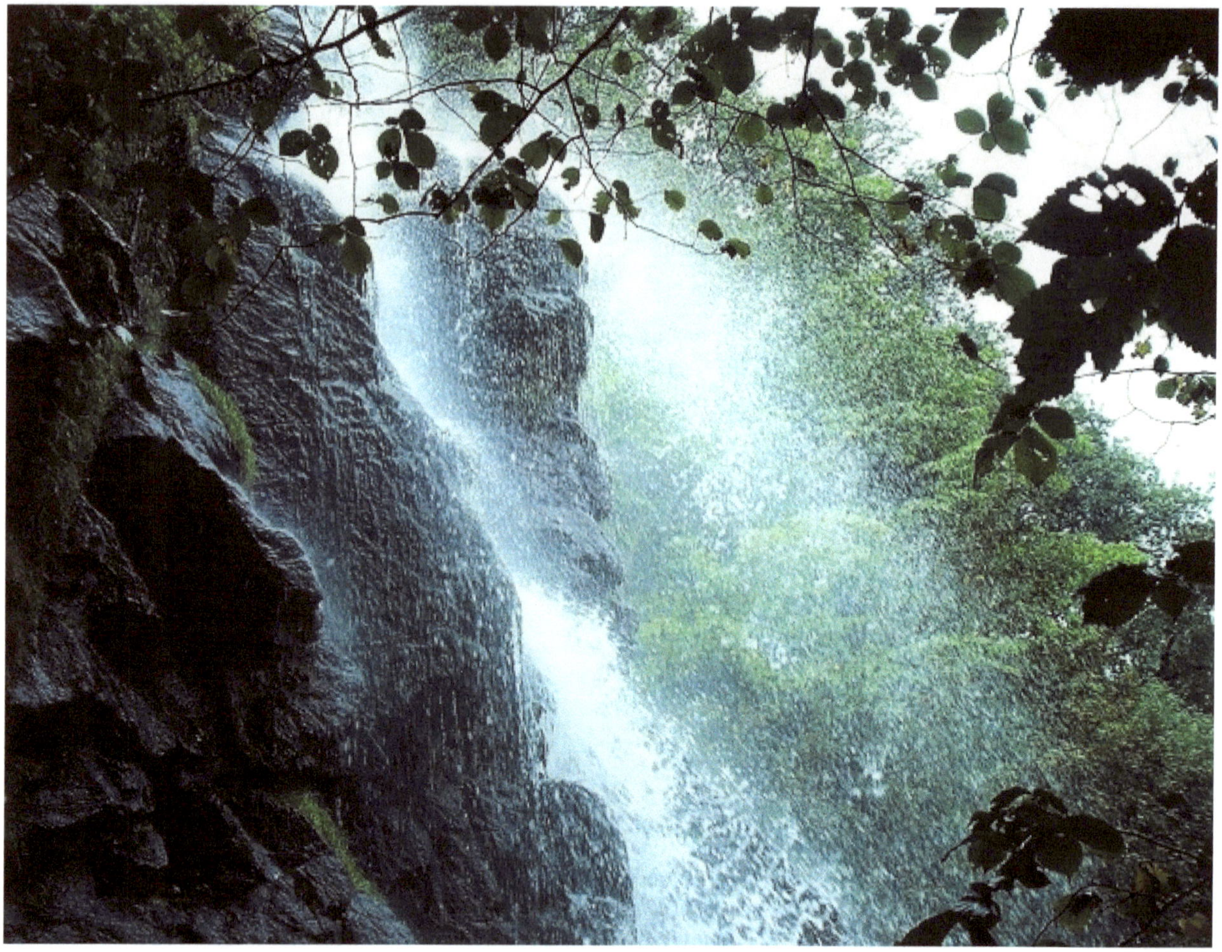

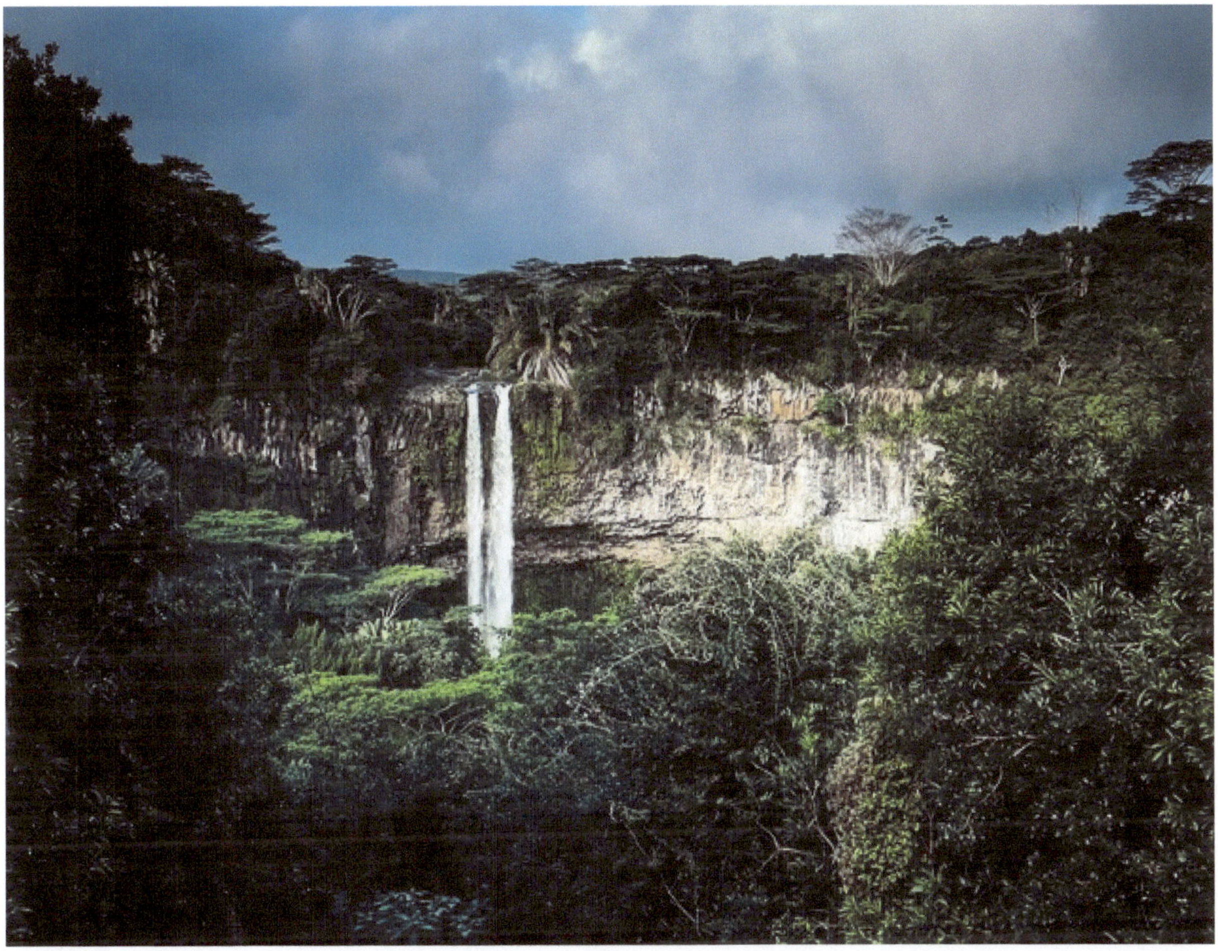

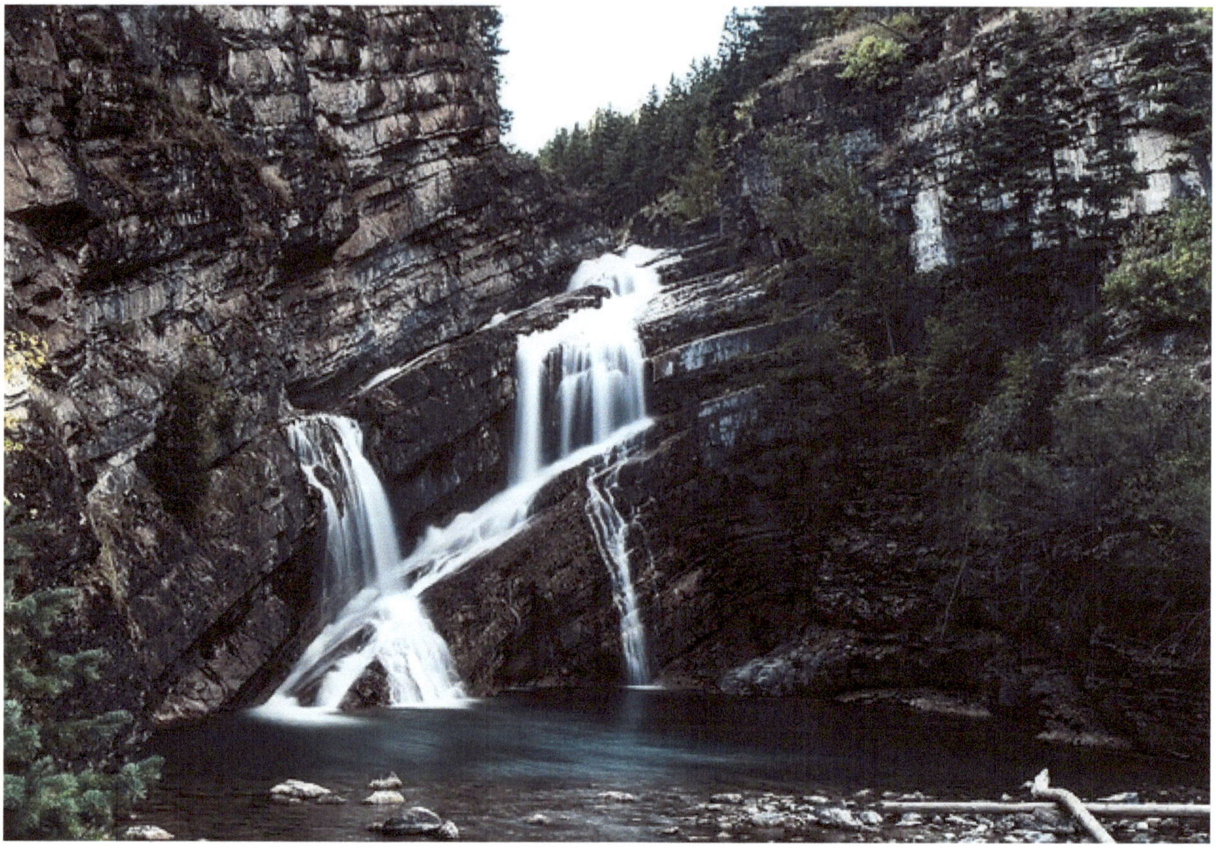

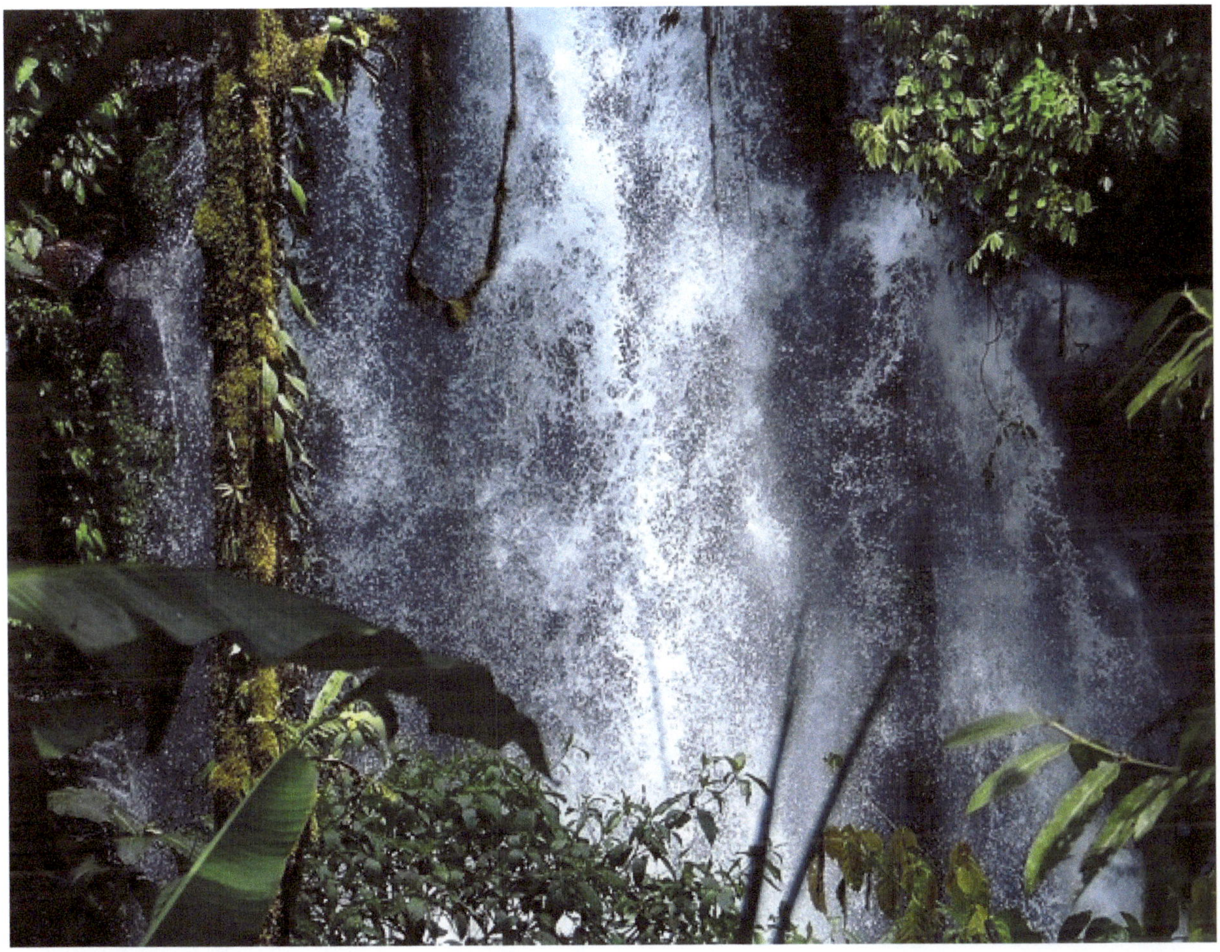

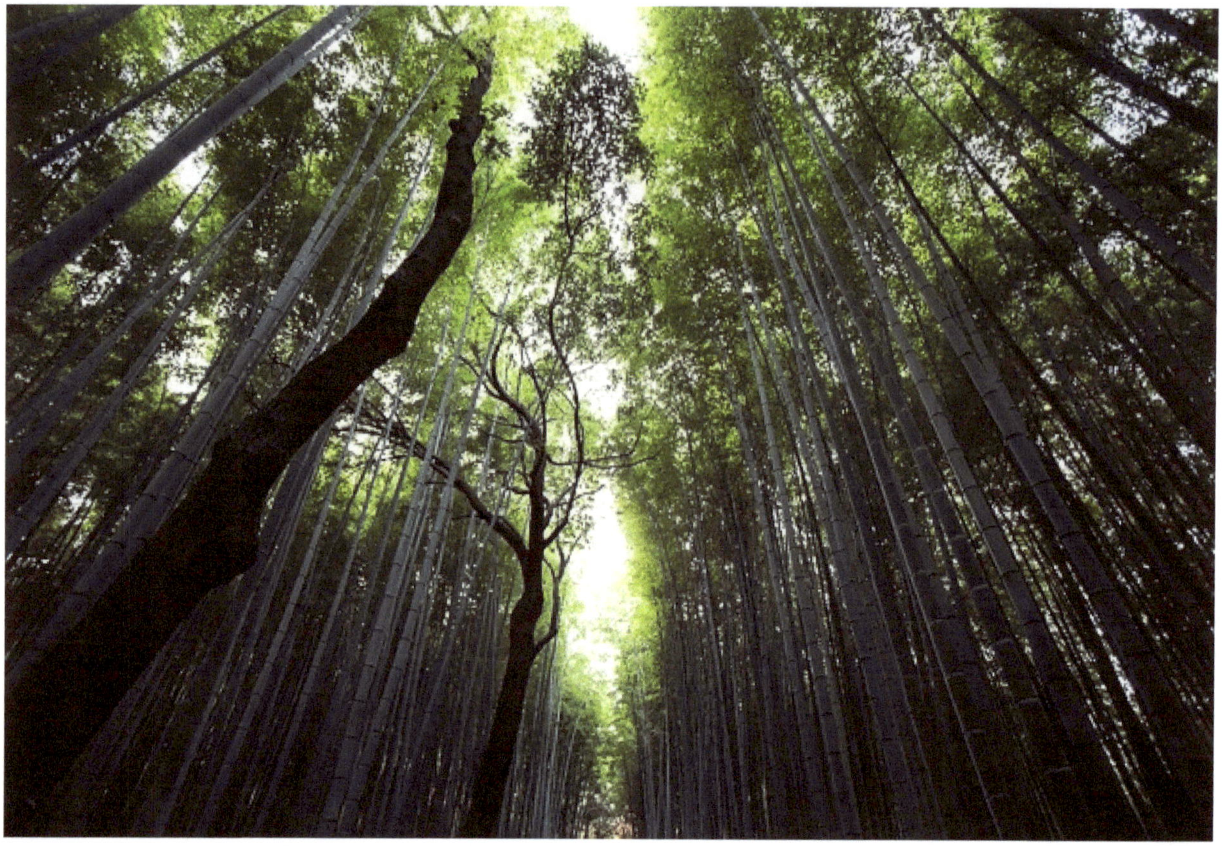

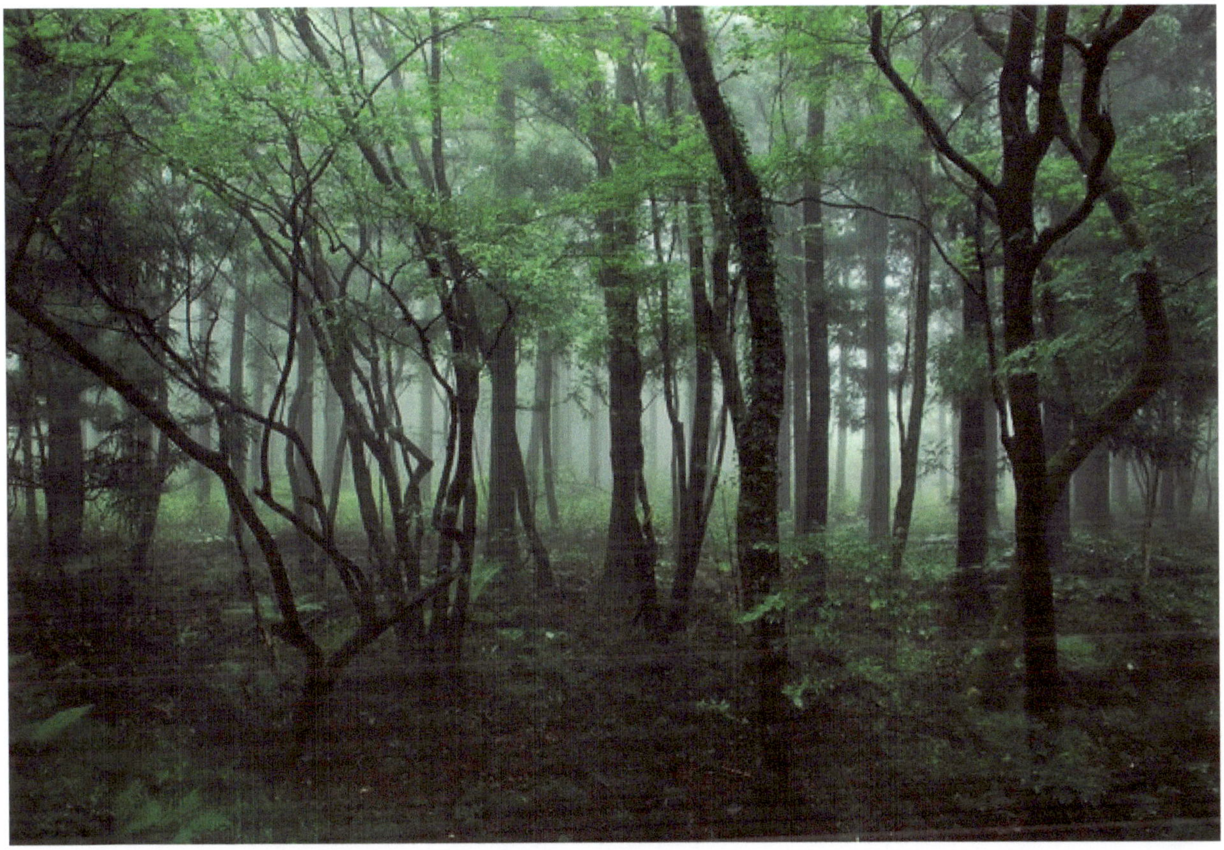

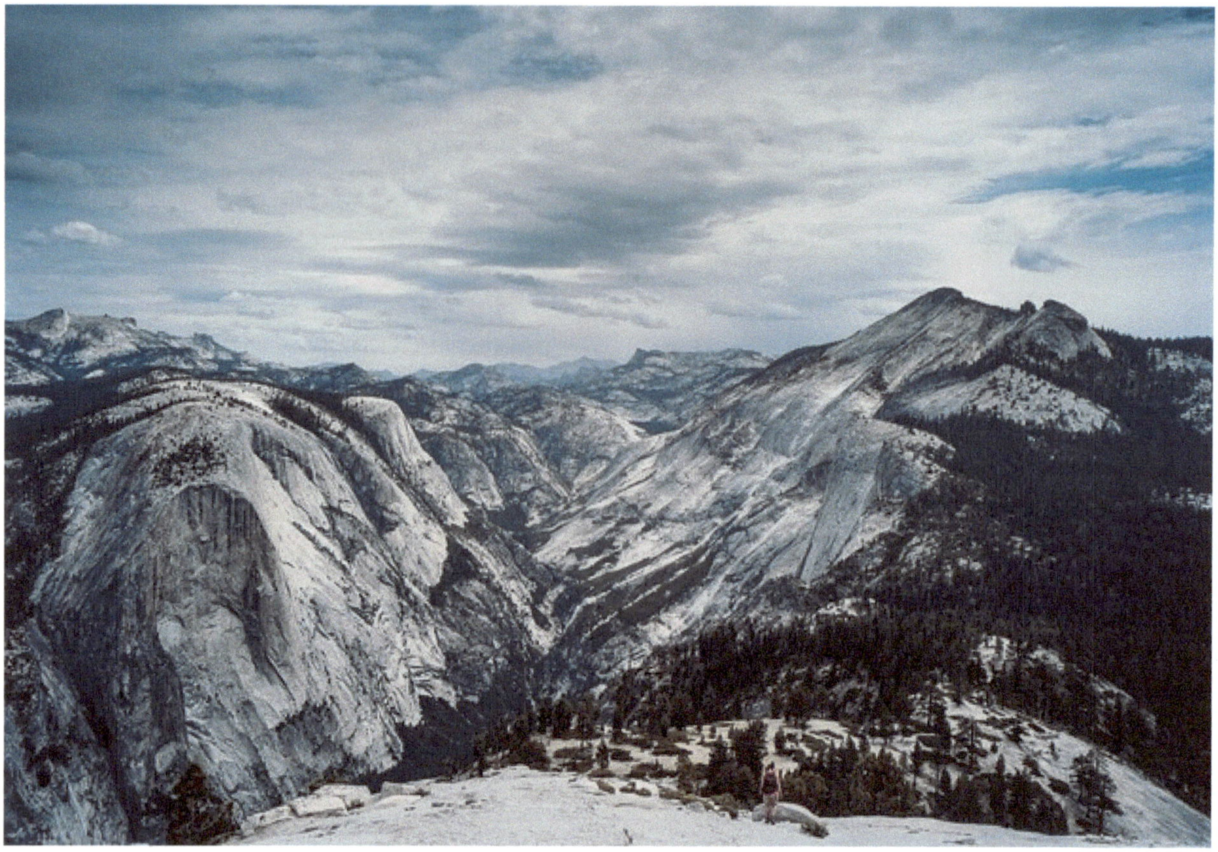

www.ingramcontent.com/pod-product-compliance
Lightning Source LLC
Chambersburg PA
CBHW060834290526
45792CB00006BB/1920
* 9 7 8 1 5 4 6 6 1 3 6 5 7 *